STRENGTH NOT SHAME

My Journey Through
Mental Health & Addiction

SHAWN FOUGÈRE

Tellwell Talent
www.tellwell.ca

ISBN
978-0-2288-7114-9 (Paperback)
978-0-2288-7115-6 (eBook)

This book is dedicated to my beautiful wife, Kathy Fougère.
She holds my heart, spirit and soul in the palm of her hand.
With her by my side, I can now walk in peace.

TABLE OF CONTENTS

Acknowledgements

Special thank you to Tamara Anderson, my illustrator and designer of my book cover art. She is an incredibly talented artist and tattooist. She can be found on Facebook @ Tattoosbytamara or via email at tattoosbytamara@gmail.com.

Thank you to the editing team and all of the professionals who contributed to publishing this book. Your faith in me and in this project is inspiring.

NIAGARA SPCA
and Humane Society

The Niagara SPCA and Humane Society was honoured to host Shawn Fougère and Kal for Shawn's first speaking engagement on his journey with PTSD. Shawn approaches a difficult topic with honesty, integrity and humour. Shawn's relationship with Kal, his wonder-dog, highlights the importance of the human-animal bond and the life-changing role of a service animal.

On behalf of the Niagara SPCA and Humane Society, we are proud of Shawn's work in transforming his journey to one of outreach and support for others. And, to all service animals near and far, this is for you.

John Greer, Executive Director
Niagara SPCA and Humane Society

About the Niagara SPCA and Humane Society

The Niagara SPCA and Humane Society is Niagara's animal charity. Our mission is to deliver innovative programs and compassionate services that enhance the lives of pets in need and the people who care for them. Together with our donors and community volunteers, we enhance lives, inspire compassion and bring joy to pets and people.

As a charity, the Niagara SPCA and Humane Society relies on donations to continue our many programs and services for animals, people and communities. We thank our donors for their generosity and welcome people and organizations to join us in support of animal well-being.

Further information about the Niagara SPCA and Humane Society can be found on the website, niagaraspca.com.

FOREWORD

───────◆•◆───────

I was quite moved when Shawn asked me to write the foreword to his book. It was an emotional moment – I felt myself tearing up. It is truly my honour to provide these few thoughts to accompany the powerful, raw, and inspiring book that he has created.

This is a very important book.

It is important because it highlights the role of systems and institutions in causing and exacerbating trauma, as well as reinforcing trauma's legacy of hopelessness and helplessness.

Shawn's raw and passionate telling of his journey provides compelling examples of institutional betrayal. Whenever he was confronted with lack of knowledge of trauma, or support for accommodation in systems of healthcare, his workplace, financial systems – there was a betrayal of trust. Trust that they would help him when he needed it. Trust that they would understand his pain and respond with compassion and empathy. When they did not, it was another layer of trauma. Layers upon layers upon layers of pain culminating in his deepest traumatic belief: that his life did not matter.

This is a call to our systems, institutions and society as a whole to be trauma-informed. I invite everyone reading this to help with this work by broadening your understanding of trauma (please see the attached Trauma Reactions and Adaptations image). Trauma is the state of hopelessness and helplessness regardless of an "event." The antidote? Compassion. Empathy. Helpful action and advocacy. It is putting person above product, power or politics.

This book is also important because it provides us, the readers, with an opportunity to dismantle our own stigmas around mental health, so we may join arms in identifying discrimination and ultimately inspire the creation of systems and a society that no longer oppresses those like Shawn, who have been willing to lay down their lives for our safety. Isn't this the least we could do for our police officers and other first responders?

To the people who have similar lived experiences to Shawn: Your life matters.

There is no one way to heal. Often, as it was for Shawn, it is a collection of loving beings (both 2-legged and 4-legged), tips and tricks for coping, everyday experiences, and therapies for moving traumatic material from one part of the brain to another (such as EMDR: eye movement desensitization and reprocessing). It is living one moment at a time. One breath at a time. Eventually, it is finding meaning in the pain. I genuinely believe that Shawn's public speaking and now writing are part of that important "meaning-making" process. How fortunate for us all.

PTSD and addiction are not life sentences.

To the people who love someone who is living with PTSD and/or substance use: Your life matters.

Your relationships have changed because of PTSD and/or substance use. That person you love is hardwired for protection, impacting your connection. There may be loss and grief.

Further, we have a neurological basis of empathy called "mirror neurons." When someone yawns, we yawn. When someone bumps their arm, we rub ours. When someone has PTSD, the amygdala and nervous systems are mis-calibrated. They sense danger and are reacting almost all the time. It's like a live wire is blowing in the wind, shorting out with every slight breeze. When a person with PTSD is someone you love and are in close contact with, your mirror neurons naturally do as they are meant to, and you pick up on their nervous system. Your own nervous system can become charged as well, like that live wire. It's natural; it's how our brains are designed to function. It is called vicarious trauma (though there can be primary and secondary trauma as well, depending on what is happening). It is real, and there is help for you, too, to soothe and recalibrate your nervous system and heal from these traumas.

To Shawn, thank you for reaching out to me. For welcoming me to join your team. I am proud to be here with you and truly honoured to have been given this space to set the stage for your readers to join your journey as they read your words.

To Kathy, I am speechless. Your love, dedication, and firm "line drawing in the sand" for Shawn is truly inspirational to read.

To the entire Fougère family, including Kal, the wonder dog, your journey has not been easy, but you all banned together through the pain, and together you will heal.

This book will have a life of its own. It will undoubtedly reach people and places that you will never truly know, even in your wildest dreams. Bravo, brave warriors.

Brenda Quenneville, MSW, RSW
Centered Fire Counselling and Consulting

Prologue

Where'd You Get To?

Walking into a dark wooded trail in the middle of the night provided a great opportunity to look to the skies and ask, where am I and how did I get where I am at this moment? The humidity has been ridiculous this year, but at nightfall, it breaks just enough to not be such a nuisance. A small warm breeze wafts through the trees and against my face and hair. I am starting to see a little clearer now as my eyes adjust to the dark. As I stand on the fringe of the City of North Bay, just far enough to eliminate the glow of the city and the noise pollution of a population of people, my senses come alive, or at the very least, I can recognize them. I can hear the serenading of the frogs, the occasional woot of an owl, and the rustling of the leaves in the trees. As I squint to sharpen my vision down the trail, I can smell nature; the forest, different plants and even the humidity.

These woods are not a scary place. I have barely left 'civilization' and I am not concerned at all for my safety or any sort of spooky or dangerous animals. The only feeling that will not go away is the feeling within me of utter confusion: how did my life spin its way and ultimately evolve to who I am and where I currently stand? What decisions did I make, did society make, did my Higher Power make, did my loved ones and friends make to mould this 40 something-year-old man?

I wonder why I am talking to myself in whispers within my own head. There are times when I scream within my skull as well; no one other than me can hear it. My voice radiating in my mind can be so dramatic, conflicted, ridiculous and mean. Not today though, today it is whispering questions, questions that are summoning a darkness from the depths of my past. The whispers are faint, but what I hear clearly is: what is hate? I am trying to define hate so that I can determine if it is, in fact, hate that I feel for myself. I imagine 'hate' to mean total disgust and loathing for something or someone, with no redeeming qualities or value. What a harsh word. Is it hate that is festering or is it rage?

I know what the brain looks like. I have seen the skull caps of many dead people sawed off. That is not an expression either. The flesh is cut around the head with a sharp scalpel, and the hair and face are peeled back to expose the skull. A power saw is then used to cut away a full chunk of the skull to expose the brain. The saw sounds like a saw, but the smell of bone is far different from wood. As you watch the skull cap pop off like the top of a jack 'o lantern, your own mind is balancing the science of the procedure with the fact that someone's face was just peeled away and their head cut open to reveal their dead brain. The brain is the command centre of your body, yet it looks like a greyish jelly mould. The brain is taken out, the stem and jelly mould parts are examined visually then put on a scale to weigh it. Now they take it and start to slice it, examinations are done, a piece is put in formaldehyde and saved. So how does this mass literally control you and encompass who and what you are?

As my visions switch from the sliced brain back to my original thought, I stand transfixed, and continue to ask, do I hate myself or am I enraged? If so, why? Either way, I ask myself why has my life come to be such a blazing blend of neurological receptor explosions, fits of hate, confusion, alcoholism, anger and resentments, combined with a basic instinct to love my family, follow my spiritual beliefs and balance the scale of what is wrong or right. Or more importantly, which of these hideous emotions can I act out and which ones will send me to jail. Or worse, to my grave. It all comes down to the jelly mould inside my skull. Did one of the many receptor explosions screw with it? Did what I have seen and felt up to this point distort what were once "normal" paths in my brain, and now they run amuck like the stagger of a drunk toddler? There are plenty of experts of the mind and brain that are smarter than me when it comes to these questions. What I do know is that hate and rage are percolating within me!

I know that it was not always the case. I still have clear memories of my youth, my wedding day, the births of my children; all typical happy days. While still visible and decipherable, they are in the background, with the hate, the rage and the haze, standing clearly in front of them and in full control of my brain. The sadness and despair are the symptoms, and being in constant pain and in a state of constant battle with the darkness is the typical result, followed by a rapid drinking binge to numb.

With absolutely no formal education or knowledge of the brain I imagine, or at the very least try to simplify or dumb down the process of how it works. The bush line is offering me a deep sense of cover from the world. When I look behind and to each side, I see the forest; in front of me is a body of water. I sit on a flattened rock just inside the tree line and realize I have zoned out again on my inner whispered dialogue. When I get these moments where my brain lets me rest and stays quiet, I appreciate them. I call them my clarity moments. My clarity moments remind me or give me hope that my brain is not totally dysfunctional and that just maybe the paths of peace from my past can be aligned and support the drunk toddler, holding their hand until they sober up and walk properly.

I think I know where the hate comes from and why I turn its venom inward. I have worked hard over the years with a few brain doctors. With their help and treatment, which includes some brain candy (aka – medication), I have progressed. The issue that I need to keep working on is to stop self-hatred. You see, every time I make progress in treatment and support is given to the tipsy toddler, it is me that gives him another drink. I keep getting in my own way. I am now creating the hate that is tearing at my soul and affecting my brain. I need to get out of my own way. It is because I am beginning to see how to help myself, but yet continue to fail miserably at doing just that. The hate continues to live rent-free in my brain, obscuring and pushing out the good. I then regard myself as an idiot, feeding the hatred and rage which further diverts me down the path of shadows.

As I sit in a safe place, I am going to let my mind go. I am going to try and introduce triggers which are painful memories from actual events and try to make sense of the paths each thought, action, sound, smell, and interaction takes. Before I close my eyes, I try and ground myself by feeling the earth around the rock, touching and peeling back the leaves from a nearby branch. I then smell the leaves on my fingers; it is a familiar smell, a pleasant smell. As I look across the beach clearing to the water, my eyes close shut, and my mind fires up. I am purposely trying to experience the past events in order to get a grip on why it is still controlling me. I am immediately frustrated because my brain is not allowing me to focus on one event in an organized fashion; it starts to shotgun blast rapid and numerous pieces of events, flashes of trauma. I open my eyes and call myself an asshole; out loud. I am mad that I cannot even concentrate on the most vivid of memories in a strategic manner for the purpose of helping myself heal. So, I chug another Cold Shot and chase it with a swig of vodka.

With that, I know that I feel hate, and more importantly, I know that it starts with hating me. I have been battling this injury for over a decade. The doctors, the specialists, the treatment centre and the independent physicians have all given my injury an official diagnosis – Post Traumatic Stress Disorder (PTSD). I have hidden my injury, I have drunk to numb my injury, I have asked for help in treating my injury, I have attempted suicide to end the pain from my injury, and I have exposed and bared the deepest and most intimate parts of my soul to treat my injury. And yet it is still not healed. It is better thanks to a lot of hard work, a loving and supporting family, some great doctors, and a highly skilled and special German Shepard named, Kal.

This is my story. The story of a northern Ontario boy who became a police officer, for God's honest truth, so that he could help people. I would never have believed how twisted, angry, drunk, pathetic, anxious and fearful I was going to become. They say that fear and anger are basically the same responses to any situation, just a different emotion, but inside, the pain is the same. I believe that to be true because while I show and demonstrate anger and rage on the outside, I am scared of the emotions on the inside. I can also tell you that when my guard drops either intentionally during a treatment session or as an exasperated puddle of an emotional mess, I cry hard, an out-of-control cry that ends with a pounding headache, an empty box of tissues followed by extreme fatigue. It is a tale that envelops and marries trauma, mental illness, addiction, policing, family and a whole lot of white-knuckled events that should have, almost have, and most certainly will kill me unless I continue to battle.

Path to Becoming a Police Officer

Have you ever had a dream to be do something so bad that you were totally committed; that it was all that you wanted? That is how I felt about becoming a police officer with the Ontario Provincial Police (OPP). It all started during a career day in grade 8 at St. Theresa's School in my hometown of Timmins, Ontario. There were various industries and companies represented, but I was in awe of a Corporal with the Ontario Provincial Police. He was sharply dressed, very witty and commanded the room just by his mere presence. What really stood out was that despite his presence and the obvious authority of his position, he acted in a very-regular-person sort of way. He took the edge off the uniform and was suddenly approachable; human, if you will. He described the career in all its glory, ranging from patrolling our highways to helping those who were injured or victimized, investigating crimes and finding people who were lost or missing. I cannot recall every detail of it as it was a few decades ago now, but I can still feel the overwhelming sense of who I would become. From that moment, I had decided that I was going to be a police officer with the Ontario Provincial Police and be just like Corporal (Cpl.) Marcel Belanger of the South Porcupine OPP. I knew then that I wanted to help people, either because they were vulnerable, injured or simply needed some direction. I wanted to make a difference in the lives of people who needed to be helped. That dream never left me, and my drive to succeed fueled my passion.

It is funny that it was Cpl. Belanger that inspired this passion and career choice because I was living with and being raised by an OPP officer, my father, Carson Fougère. I knew what he did for a living, but during my youth, he was working in crime units and dressed either in a suit or more commonly, in regular average Joe-type clothing as a Detective. I can even remember and have seen pictures of him when I was younger with long hair and looking unkempt as he played his role in solving crime by fitting into the culture of the time. He did not drive a police car, but he drove issued police vehicles like pick-up trucks, panel vans and my personal favourite, a 2 door Chevrolet Monte Carlo. Another reason I did not see the OPP officer in him every day was because when he was at home, he was my father and did not bring his work home. I did not see a police officer, nor was there a culture of it at my house. My dad had a gift of being able to be a great police officer as well as a great father; keeping them separate was just who he was. I envy him. A funny sidebar, though, I remember overhearing my parents talking one day. We were planning on spending the Canada Day long weekend at our cottage on Kenogamissi Lake, and they were discussing a possible leaving time. I heard him tell my mother that our leaving time would depend on whether or not a particular outlaw motorcycle gang arrived in Timmins. If the bikers arrived in the city before Friday, the weekend would be cancelled, but if they came afterwards, we were good to go. My parents discussed this as though this were a normal, everyday reason why a family vacation might need to be delayed. I still chuckle that he was able to be that fun dad, taking us water skiing and fishing in one moment, and then able to switch in one phone call, entering the world of bikers and organized crime. I was very fortunate growing up, I had a mother and a father that were attentive caregivers, great teachers and created a supportive atmosphere for my sister and I to learn and grow.

I was hell-bent on becoming a member of the OPP. I put all my eggs in one basket, and enrolled in the Law and Security Administration Program at my college. It was a great program if you were going to be a police officer but did nothing else if your goals were not achieved. I requested ride-alongs with different patrol officers on my own time as well as part of my school curriculum. I studied the phonetic alphabet and all the 10 codes used by the OPP, before I had applied or even graduated. I was focused.

Once I graduated from college, my application went in, and the long process began. This was in 1991, and the government was focused, as it should have been, on increasing diversity and equity. Having equal representation of the police in relation to the population just makes sense. Having officers on the force able to empathize with those who may feel a little different can really go a long way to connecting with individuals in the community. I, myself have a stutter – which is considered a speech impediment. To be honest, I've never had an issue with it. The way I saw it, and still do, is that the stutter actually makes me unique, and I often use it as a form of humour and as a way to break the ice when meeting new people or out with friends. I knew the competition would be tough but I was more than committed to working for it – I was also French-speaking so I had that going for me. I didn't know this at the time, but this was the first time I would see the power and influence that societal expectations can have on the legislation of common sense, fairness, and simply doing what is right. There will be more on this throughout this book, but my point now is to illustrate my journey to the badge. After begrudgingly listing my stuttering as a disability on my application form, I began their process. The process entailed the application, a written test, psychological questionnaires, a vision test, interview, fitness testing, background checks and then finally, a job offer. It was quite the process. I recall failing the written test the first time, primarily in the area of math. Of all the stages I thought would be difficult, the written test was not it. This setback cost me a year as that was who long I had to wait to re-apply.

While I was waiting out my dead time, the OPP was hiring 2 contract civilians for the role of dispatcher in the North Bay Communications Centre. I applied and was successful. As a side note, I really enjoyed my time as a dispatcher. I worked with a great group of people, and while the job was very difficult and hectic at times, the crew there made it enjoyable, and we shared many laughs and good times. I was not able to mentally submerge myself in this role as my focus was to become a police officer, and this job was a stepping stone. Before some dispatchers read this and get upset, my term 'stepping stone' related to my specific journey to the badge only. The dispatcher, especially in today's climate, is an incredibly difficult job; a job I know can suck the life out of you just as it does for the members on the road. I was a dispatcher from May 1992 to December 31, 1993.

After my dead time expired, the application went back in. This time I was successful through the written tests and right up to the fitness testing. For whatever reason, the OPP and the Ontario Police College felt that in order to prove you were physically fit, you had to run a mile and a half in certain time ranges based on age and sex. They had other tests such as push-ups, ab tests and flexibility, but this run meant everything. When I was completing this testing, I was ripped. I had just finished playing Junior 'A' hockey, was 22 years old and strong as an ox. I was 5'10" and 210 lbs, with no belly fat in sight. My problem was that my running style was that of a club-footed bear. I could not run long distances. It had nothing to do with my wind, it was that my stride was not smooth, and my shins, knees and lower back took a beating within the first 5 minutes. I could ace the other part of the testing, and despite my obvious fitness level, if I couldn't jog, I'd fail. Now, I have been a police officer for 25 years, and I have worked with members who could jog 10 kilometres without breaking a sweat. Some of these "runners" were about as fit as a dampened feather, but they could run, eh! My point is, in 25 years, I have never seen a police officer in full kit run after a bad guy at a consistent pace with proper stride length for a mile and a half. That is what the car is for, and if they run away out of sight, we call in our puppy (i.e., Police K-9) who is more than eager to track them down. It was so frustrating. I did not complete the mile and a half run in the allotted time, so I failed that portion. I finished it, but not sufficiently according to their damn charts. I was able to have another crack at the fitness testing.

I sought out the help of two current OPP members at the time (Daryl Foulkes and Alex Zapotocnzy) who were not only fit and strong but were fantastic runners. With the help of these two, I began to run 5 kilometres, focusing on stride and technique, over and over again. One of those guys actually ran backwards in front of me while I was thumping forward to critique my style. With great thanks to these two, I passed the fitness test and completed the run in the allotted time. These fitness criteria were not practical whatsoever in relation to the job as a police officer, but because I ran really well I could move on. The fitness testing used now is a fantastic measure of strength, endurance and flexibility, and does relate to what could be expected of you on the street as a police officer. In my opinion, it was a change for the better.

On January 3, 1994, I reported to the OPP Provincial Academy in Brampton, Ontario, to begin one week of orientation, followed by 12 weeks of schooling and training at the Ontario Police College (OPC) in Aylmer, Ontario, followed by three more weeks at the OPP Provincial Academy to learn the OPP way of business. During my stay at the latter, we were shown para-military type discipline, including ensuring our beds were made according to the all-important hospital corner tuck. We were awoken at 5:00 am to run out on the streets of Brampton, followed by a full day of class, and ending the day with an evening of drill practice by a want-to-be Drill Sergeant. It was, in fact, a great experience overall. It was here where I learned the pride of the uniform, the duties of a police officer and started to feel like my journey to reaching my goal was almost complete. I received confirmation that I would be posted to the Parry Sound Detachment, and I was excited. I knew from dispatching this detachment that they were busy and provided an equal amount of highway and traffic experience, as well as a Municipal policing element that I was looking forward to.

We had a large graduation ceremony at OPC. Our families were invited to watch the spectacle and transformation of new police recruits. My mom and dad were there as well as my future parents-in-law and my girlfriend, Kathy. I concocted a plan for my graduation. A plan that would need the approval of the Director of the OPC, as well as the Solicitor General of Ontario, who would be in attendance on that day. I decided that I wanted to propose to Kathy and ask her to marry me in front of everyone. Let me set the stage for you here. The Drill Hall at OPC is huge, at least 1 and ½ times the size of a hockey arena. There were about 300 recruits graduating that day from police agencies from all over Ontario, their families, dignitaries and of course a pipe and drum band; no pressure. I received all of the approvals, and everyone was a buzz. It was funny on the day of the graduation to see my classmates and others who were in the know look at Kathy as I introduced them before the ceremony; they were giddy with excitement. I was pretty pumped, too, as well as wanting to vomit. What the hell was I thinking.

All of the new recruits were broken down into mini-classes during our training at OPC. Each class consisted of 2 Sergeants who were our instructors and about 25 to 30 of us students. My plan, which involved my entire class, began with the Master of Ceremony calling my class up to the front just before the ceremony was to start. As a class, you are taught during drill sessions how to line up in rank formation, march, salute etc. So, when the call was made, led by our Sergeants, my class marched in formation to the front of the room, near the stage of dignitaries and formed our ranks. In order for this plan to work it was integral that I came up with a reason for Kathy to be up front. I had told Kathy that before the ceremony, I was receiving a special award as a result of my training excellence and needed her to come to the front of the crowd with my camera to capture the big event. Kathy was a very shy girl and wanted to decline the duties and pass the camera off to a family member. I really needed to work my charm and tell her how important it was that she see and capture my accomplishment firsthand. As my class stood in formation, the entire crowd not knowing what the hell was going on, my Sergeant yelled my name to come forward. In my best march possible, I crept towards the front of my class in front of my Sergeant. Now Kathy was at the front, but kind of hiding behind other photographers. I smiled at her, and she prepped the camera. I reached into my front dress tunic pocket and grabbed the ring box. There were close to 1000 people in the hall, yet for that moment, none of them were there. I knew that in that small box was a ring I had personally designed and had made by Roger's Jewellers in North Bay. The engagement ring formed an 'S' shape (for Shawn) lined with diamond chips, and once the wedding day occurred, it would fit into the 'S' shaped wedding band topped with a diamond. I was wearing those cloth white gloves you see during these types of ceremonies, making it very hard to grip the felt ring box. Once I secured the ring in my hand, I ordered my class, like a drill sergeant would, to drop to one knee. My entire class went down to a knee. I followed and opened the box. I was shaking so much it felt like the entire floor was heaving. I opened the ring box, looked at Kathy, and she looked at me. She, like most of the crowd, was trying to process what the hell was happening. Right about at the same time as Kathy clued in, the crowd did as well, and some squeals and deep sighing could be heard. I remember saying, "Kathy, I love you, will you marry me?" She just started to cry and gave me a big hug and buried her face in the crook of my neck and shoulder, and the crowd roared and clapped with excitement. We were in a deep embrace; people were cheering, and I still had not heard her say yes. I made her look at me through the excitement and the noise and said, "So?" And she said, "Yes, yes." Now I graduate as an engaged man.

After that graduation, I headed to the Provincial Academy for 3 more weeks of learning OPP policy, records management etc., followed by my full graduation and badge presentation as a police officer with the Ontario Provincial Police. I had family gathered and was really excited. Not only because I was getting my badge, but because it is OPP tradition that if you have a family member as a member of the OPP, they can give you your badge. I am so close to my dad and so very proud of him that I could not wait for him to present me with my badge. Well, some rocket scientist managed to ruin this moment for quite a few of us.

There were just over 120 OPP recruits graduating, the largest graduating class the OPP had had to date. The plan was that they would have 3 lines handing out the badges. I remember that the Commissioner of that day, Thomas O'Grady was one of them, and our Deputy Commissioner Nagle was the 2nd one. I was so upset and hurt during the badge presentation that I do not even remember who the third one was. The brain trusts of the organizing committee told my father, a Commissioned Officer, Superintendent and a District Commander in the East Region, that he could not present me with my badge. I was informed that one of the main reasons for this was because organizing the recruits during the presentations would be too complicated due to the large number of recruits. In addition, Deputy Commissioner Nagle insisted that she present the badges to the female officers. They felt that the logistics would be too complicated to form a 4th line for family members and were afraid the event would become too long. Are you kidding me? The way it went was we were told that our names would be called up alphabetically and would be directed to a line at that time. That does not sound all that complicated to me, and furthermore, wouldn't adding a fourth line speed up the ceremony? How hard would it have been to ensure the recruits with family members presenting a badge went to the family line. I was furious, sad and really hurt. My dad was furious and actually made a complaint about it, but alas, what seemed simple to my father and I was viewed as too difficult by those making the decisions. As a result, I, along with numerous others were robbed of a very special and meaningful moment. I even recall that the daughter of the Chief of Toronto Police of the day,

Bill McCormack, was graduating in my class, and they too could not experience that special moment. We are still the only class ever denied the opportunity to experience this monumental event. I remember the day well, our want-to-be Drill Sergeant (who was promoted up to Chief Superintendent), and some of his cronies were running around in quite a fuss. I was furious. I couldn't understand how calling names and handing out a piece of metal in front of family and friends could be so difficult. There was no compromise. The command was given by the higher up and it seemed the organizers were more worried about their own careers instead of the ones just starting. What they should have done was focus on the experience for the recruit and that everything was properly prepared and more relaxed. So, for one final time – whoever made the decision to rob me and others out of a special moment, especially the excitement I had for 17 weeks during training to see my dad's tearing eyes during our special moment, from my perspective, you were incompetent. I digress.

A few days after graduation, I reported to the Parry Sound Detachment with a fellow recruit from my class. I was fit, excited, my uniform and boots polished, and I could not wait to begin my career.

Changes in Policing from 1992 to Now

---◆●◆---

I remember speaking with my Sergeant one day following a yearly weekend festival that was always a shit show. Large groups of people flocked to our area every year to party, celebrate, be entertained, drink, and drug their faces off. I heard the saying once that the police spend 90% of their time dealing with 10% of the population, and that is fairly accurate, in my opinion. We were all beat after 3 days and nearly finished for another year. This Sergeant had organized logistics and personnel for a number of years and was always in amongst the crowds even though he was crowding on 30 years' service. I asked him how he dealt with this chaos, repeated behaviour and potential eruptions of unrest. His answer was typical – "that's what alcohol is for."

When I put the uniform on starting in April of 1994, I know now just how pure and naïve I was. At the time, I didn't think so. I grew up around police officers, and the older I became, the more conversations I had with 'the boys' about what they did. I heard the veterans telling me their tales, spicing it up and creating stories of drama an old fisherman would be proud of. I knew some people stole, hurt one another, did drugs, broke traffic laws, hated the police, committed suicide, died suddenly, or were even murdered. I saw the news and was equipped with the knowledge through readings, research, study, and the experience told from others. I saw and watched my fellow officers over a coffee or a beer relay and describe funny, tragic, humorous and sometimes horrible tales of calls they had been on or investigations they went through. I watched how animated they were, reliving events and almost bragging of who saw the most, did the most and kicked ass the most. What I saw through my eyes and absorbed as a 23-year-old rookie police officer was just how tough these guys and gals were. What I saw was an example of who I was to be. I did not once hear an officer describe how sad a fatal collision had made them feel or how the death of a child or a sexual assault investigation kept them up at night. I did not hear that from my peers; I was not taught that in training, it was not discussed by my managers, and I did not know of any outlets available to support police officers in dealing with these feelings. Twenty-five years ago, I was given to understand that as police officers, we are able to handle anything in-house. No one felt haunted, anxious, scared, sad, preoccupied, disturbed or needing to ask – "what is wrong with the world"? No, what I saw was a group of police officers that answered the call, shift after shift. I heard and saw nothing that indicated that what we experienced, witnessed, dealt with or were exposed to impacted the police officer negatively or injured their mental wellness.

The regime of my rookie years seemed to be built on a brotherhood/sisterhood with an us-against-the-world mentality. The group of officers I was learning from were senior and had a wealth of information and knowledge. Our shifts were busy, but we were always there for one another, on and off duty. I believe this tight-knit camaraderie was what kept everyone going to answer the call. When we were at work, we worked hard even when busy and sometimes with shorthanded staff. What I remember most with the group of officers in Parry Sound was the humour and the laughter amongst one another. When we were off duty, we all hung out together as well. I cannot speak for the older officers, but not knowing a soul in this small community, other than my colleagues, made life a little difficult to adjust to as a rookie. It is one of the few occupations where you apply for employment and then have no idea where they are going to send you. Your first posting is often away from home, family and friends. When I moved to Parry Sound, I was alone in that regard, but so many of the officers took me under their wings and often included me in extracurricular activities. I feel fortunate to have started in a community such as Parry Sound. The workload was steady, with a great variety of calls for service, in an extremely beautiful town, and the Detachment members were outstanding in teaching and guiding me in my new career. The Detachment at that time was described by some as being very busy, and rookies that started there learnt by baptism by fire and either learned to swim fast or surely sink. I loved it there.

What started to become perfectly clear right from the very start was that my perception of the world and what I believed were characteristics of a bad guy were not even close. The normal, everyday calls, were as I thought they would be. It was some of the violent calls, the brutal victimization with a lack of any remorse, and what horrendous crashes can do to the human body that opened my eyes wider than I knew they could go. I had no idea how evil some people could be. I am not about to go into a "look at what I suffered through" type of log of events. It is my opinion that how any person processes trauma and what even constitutes trauma is personal in nature and cannot be judged as yes; it is, or no; it is not, by anyone else. In addition to the images burnt in my mind are the memories of the actual victims of crime. The way I was processing their pain took a toll on me, and it consumed me as well. You will recall I mentioned earlier that I became a police officer because I wanted to help people. It was that very personal trait that was the root of so much of my pain; suffering with no mechanism for coping or even a place to talk about it.

My personality and how I treat people, in my opinion, make me a caring police officer. I am not patting myself on the back at all. It is what it is. I excel at taking statements from and working with victims or witnesses, and spending time with them. I have compassion, patience and have even cried with some and always ensure they are comfortable and ok after their police interaction. On the other side of the coin, I do not necessarily possess the skills to question/interrogate an accused like others officers. My demeanour of empathy and caring very rarely works with an accused. They can feel I am not equipped to push the envelope, and as such, I do not tend to be very successful in obtaining the information we are generally after. There are times, however, that the victimization of a person has caused me to walk into the interview of an accused very mad and lose my composure, demanding answers right now. That rarely works either. I have noticed that the officers who have the ability to interrogate a bad guy have abilities I do not possess. They can show empathy, even play the role of understanding them and why they may have done what they did. They can spend hours with them, having a calm conversation. They have their strengths, and I have mine. They are both important, and in some cases, an officer can deliver on both counts.

Now here is my issue with the policing profession. Do my personality traits make me weaker? Does that mean there is no place in policing for a person like me? No, it does not. Having a blend of personalities, strengths and abilities is the key to any team. It is the same in policing. The difference is, in policing, if you are not a perceived bullet-proof, type 'A' rock star, then you are a wimp that 'should suck it up buttercup.' Why is that? The other thing I know is that those bullet-proof types are actually full of it at times, and do not allow themselves to show their feelings to anyone else because it is not 'proper'. Therein lies the circle of insanity.

Suppose a police officer hurts their back or ankle while at work and needs a couple of days off to recover. Why can an officer not request the same time off to rest and receive treatment for a psychological or mental health injury? I will tell you why from my experience; you will be teased, gossiped about, shamed and be deemed a wimp that should never have become a police officer in the first place. That is the core of the problem and why police officers are dying, in my opinion. The culture is flawed, and no one is addressing it properly. What I have seen, especially with what I have experienced, is that committees are formed to form sub-committees to offer verbal diarrhea to the public. I can even bring you to the infamous Ontario Ombudsman's Report, In the Line of Duty, written in 2012, on Post Traumatic Stress Disorder or Mental Injuries. Putting forth 34 recommendations, the Ontario Ombudsman's Report clearly identified the trauma suffered by people diagnosed with PTSD and how the OPP lacked in its duty to deal with PTSD. Many people do not know that I was interviewed by 2 members of the Ontario Ombudsman's office for close to 4 hours about my experience. I received a copy of that report. I believe that report was written with sincerity however, it wasn't worth the paper it was written on because it lacked any sort of teeth to bring about required change. That is the problem with the OPP and mental health stigma; there is no accountability and discipline. As a consequence, how many officers committed suicide after the Ombudsman's Report? Way too many. Police officers and civilian members alike with PTSD continue to suffer the additional burden of stigma in the police workplace.

While the OPP was processing this information, three OPP officer suicides, in August 2018, became public; Constable Joshua De Bock, age 38, Detective-Inspector Paul Horne, age 50 and Sergeant Sylvain Routhier, age 37. My heart goes out to the Officers and their families for these tragic losses of life.

In fact, just seven years after the 2012 Ontario Ombudsman's report that severely criticized the OPP and the Ministry of Community Safety and Correctional Services, Ontario's Chief Coroner, with the aid of an expert panel, conducted another review after he learned of nine police suicides in 2018.

Again, there were recommendations, not the least being that the realities of the police mental health "ecosystem" have to change; that police officers need better and clearer mental health and suicide-prevention resources.

In 2019, the CBC's The Fifth Estate aired the program Officer Down: Suicide and harassment in Ontario's provincial police service, creating awareness of the systemic problem and the toxic culture existing in the OPP. Journalist Mark Kelley reported that in the last 30 years, more OPP officers have died by suicide than in the line of duty. He went on to report that a key recommendation of the Ombudsman's was to establish a suicide prevention program. As of 2019, seven years after the Ombudsman's report, it still had not been done. The OPP continued to fail to protect its own. At the time of publishing my book, Officer Down remains available on You Tube.

What did the OPP do after the report was issued? They formed a committee. Guess what? I met with that committee too. It was an Acting Inspector and a Staff Sergeant. I travelled to Orillia from North Bay and sat with them for over 2 hours. They made tons of notes. Absolutely nothing came of it, other than more suicides. What came next was the OPP Wellness Unit. A new unit was formed, and protocols were put in place for the member to reach out and get some real help. An excellent concept, and I honestly believe it will benefit some. However, it is unlikely to benefit the members who are killing themselves because they have to reach out, and they have to put themselves out there and deal with the shame, stigma and 'suck-it-up, buttercup' effect. Even with the Wellness Unit, the OPP suffered the three member suicides in short order to one another. The Wellness Unit does not and cannot help those members because the OPP fails to address the problem.

I have said over and over again, and even to the executive members of the OPP which includes the Commissioner, Deputies and all of the Chief Superintendents, that committees do not work and are not the solution. Furthermore, committees out of Orillia General Headquarters are even worse. That is why I continue to experience frustration with the OPP; they keep forming committees out of Orillia rather than actual members, and creating acronyms for mental health solutions that are but a smokescreen. Members continue to die. How do I know that the OPP are doing nothing beneficial and do not listen to members such as me, or from the spouses of our members both struggling and dead?

Because I have told them in writing and in person. I have personally met with the Chief Superintendent in charge of our Human Resources and Accommodation Plan and told her the flaws as they relate to mental injuries. I gave her a document outlining that not only are they flawed, but they actually shun the suffering member, causing the reverse effect. The process itself is causing members to stay quiet and suffer in silence. I then met with and delivered a full one-hour PowerPoint presentation to the executive committee of the OPP in Orillia. As a sidebar, I drove to Orillia from North Bay in my own vehicle, on my own time and with my father as a support person without any compensation for expenses. Nice touch, eh? During this PowerPoint I outlined the changes that needed to be made. I told them to seek out actual members who are suffering to lead these efforts, rather forming committees out of Orillia. Not only did that fall on deaf ears, but as I mentioned above, three members unfortunately committed suicide right around that time. Also mentioned above, their response was to form another committee, this time chaired by Chief Superintendents and directed by our Criminal Investigations Bureau (CIB). They are doing a Provincial Tour as I write this book to reach out to suffering members to gain knowledge to fix the problem. It won't work for the member debating to choose life or choose death. You see, their committee is holding round table discussions at local hotels for our members. Essentially asking an already ashamed, fearful and segregated member to come to a public place, meet with their peers and tell in a public forum what they can barely discuss in a private treatment session.

Some members will go, and they will benefit from the sessions and feel supported; for that I am happy. It must be remembered that the ideas and opinions I am sharing are mine and how they have and continue to relate to my story. I could not participate; I simply could not.

I know I sound negative, and that is because I am. I am because I'm trying to help the next member from not dying. These roundtables, committees, Wellness Unit contacts are great for the members who chose to contact the numbers and reach out to the committees but do very little to prevent a member from suffering in silence or shame, and from committing suicide. You see there is only one way to help those members, to help me, and that is for an entire culture change at every rank. I will elaborate on this further in the book, but essentially what I am saying is not complicated or expensive. We need to stop trying to mandate policy changes by way of committees or rank. There needs to be an end to press conferences where we say the right things but do nothing in the background. What the members need, what I need, is for every member of the OPP, regardless of rank, uniform or civilian, to smarten up and start caring about one another. I have ideas for how this could work, but no one listens to a mentally injured Constable who has served his entire career in the North East Region of Ontario.

From 1992 to the present, I do believe we have come a long way in understanding that PTSD and mental injuries are real. I believe the public and even the odd politician understand some of the possible fatal outcomes of this injury. The problem is, the day-to-day life of an affected member is not experiencing this understanding and continues to feel the glaring eyes of judgement. I have seen news conferences where the OPP says all the right things. They say they understand striping a member of their gun or uniform can be like striping a person's identity. They say they know that no one reaches out to them, and they often sit alone. They went from being a part of the largest fraternity to sitting alone in disgrace. The OPP knows that the mentally injured cannot at times navigate through the muddy waters of accommodation, sick leave, Workplace Safety and Insurance Board (WSIB) and insurance coverage as a direct result of the injury itself. The OPP knows everything. I have heard all of the right, powerful people acknowledge the very things that are roadblocks to the member and could end the stigma around mental health. They say it; they even claim to know it, but forming a committee to form sub-committees to gather information about countless members deaths, that has been gathered before, is futile and the exact definition of insanity.

I will expand on this topic further, as it is the basis and the drive behind writing this book in the first place. My goal for this chapter was to illustrate that when I joined the OPP, it was very much a bravado-type attitude mixed with a little 'suck-it-up, buttercup' mentality. Trauma and mental illness were not trained or discussed; it was just part of the job. As I sit here 28 years later, trauma and mental illness are understood and generally accepted as real. There are training and support systems now in place for members, and all of this is a good thing. I mean that. However, the bravado, the 'accept it bitch, as part of the job' attitude, is still alive. Every civilian, front-line uniform or detective, supervisor, manager and all Commissioned Officers up to and including the Commissioner are the ones that can put a stop to it all. The question is, are the few dickheads and judgemental managers who are failing to do their job ready for what needs to be done? Let's see.

Police and Bureaucratic Nonsense

---●·●---

This chapter has been my biggest challenge. The anger and resentments I will speak about throughout this book are embedded and deeply connected to the managers of the Ontario Provincial Police. This chapter has been totally re-written and re-focused. My original thoughts and notes focused on every event where the OPP failed me. I wrote names, quoted Commissioned Officers and spewed the venom that has paralyzed my life for years. I could not get past this topic and had to stop and start writing often. Just sitting at the keyboard or scribbling notes in my journal about events, decisions, and the repetitive bullshit of it all, sent me into fits of anger, depressive states and a general feeling of low self-worth. What I was doing was reliving each of the dozens and dozens of times the OPP threw me under the bus and failed my mental health injury and conditions. It wasn't until, after such an episode of utter rage, that I finally came to understand what my direction should be. I headed out into the bush, my safe place to burn off steam and hit an internal reset. I asked myself why am I putting myself through this all over again. It struck me as clear as a bell. I wanted to write a book about my experience, strength and hope as they relate to my mental health conditions and my addiction. I wanted to share my journey so others can know that they are not alone and should never feel ashamed. The OPP managers are part of my journey, but certainly not the entire trip.

What I can now say with some relative accuracy from conversations with many others is that the OPP managers and Human Resources are pretty much the same as other Government agencies, as well as private organizations. They are not equipped to handle mental health injuries. They are so caught up in operating procedures that they fail to see the human being behind the mental health diagnosis. With over 8000 employees across the Province of Ontario, it's fair to say that the OPP is very large. Due to our size and geographical makeup, regions were determined, and rank and file were established. There is a hierarchy, or a chain of command, in each region. Each region reports to the main General Headquarters (GHQ), based out of Orillia. GHQ has been nicknamed the puzzle palace. GHQ is supposed to set out procedures in every area of human resources and policing standards, and the regions are all to fall in line. Now, there has to be some latitude for discretion as a result of geographical differences and community representation. What works in the Greater Toronto Region may not be the proper policy to follow at the Hearst Detachment in Northern Ontario, for example. That just makes sense. However, as with anything involving this model of silo villages, little empires begin to develop. What comes out of GHQ is not necessarily followed across the regions, some use the discretionary latitude to their advantage.

To explain where I have fallen within the rank-and-file structure of the OPP, I will breakdown what my chain of command looked like from the eyes of a constable.

When I worked at a Detachment within a region on the front-line, either as a road officer responding to calls for service or in the Crime Unit, my silo was relatively small. The constable is at the bottom of the food chain with respect to the uniform sworn members. The constable works within a platoon or a unit and reports to a sergeant. The sergeant, in theory, is the constable's only go to for everything from vacation requests, notification of crimes protocols, calling in sick, requesting specialized services such, as an Identification Unit at a crime scene or a technical collision officer at a fatal or major crash, etc. That sergeant then reports to the detachment commander which is generally a staff sergeant. There are inspector run detachments as well, for larger areas, but I never worked at a detachment with that structure. That's it. Keep in mind there are usually four sergeants for the four platoons, a detective sergeant for the Crime Unit, and if the detachment is really flush, there is an administrative sergeant that oversees and reports to the staff sergeant in a support role. As for me, the constable, my chain of command is to my assigned sergeant. The staff sergeant may be approachable to assist in the event of a conflict, but other than staff sergeant Gord Kingshott at my first posting in Parry Sound, my North Bay staff sergeants were not. Finally, the detachment staff sergeant reports the goings-on from their silo to the larger regional silo, through their assigned inspector or superintendent.

It was in 2005, while I was a front-line constable out of the North Bay detachment that I was no longer able to suppress the issues I was experiencing. At that time, the detachment commander / staff sergeant was probably the worst manager I have ever had to report to. He was removed as the detachment commander and moved to region headquarters in a role where he would not be responsible for managing anyone. In my opinion, he lacked the ability to lead and communicate with other people. He was a smart man, just an absolute asshole to deal with. He sat in the penalty box for a few years but then managed to join the crew within the inner circles of region and was promoted to a commissioned officer as an inspector. One of his roles was as the inspector in charge of Human Resources for the entire North East region. Here is a perfect example of the head-scratching decisions that went on. It was common chatter among front line members and detachment staff that the region commanders removed him as a staff sergeant of a detachment of 50 or so employees, primarily as a result of many complaints and obvious issues with respect to his leadership and inability to manage other humans, so they then promoted him to an executive position as an Inspector thus giving him his commission, and he was now the manager of all Human Resources in the entire region, about 650+ employees. I digress.

I could literally write a series of books just on the Human Resources gurus, executive and uniform managers explaining how they not only failed to help me, but belittled, shamed and beat me down to a shell of a man. Some were simply not trained or lacked the skills required to think outside the box and blaze a new path for members suffering from mental injuries. The other managers only thought about themselves and how to get ahead and get their friends there, too. In the North East region, for a time, if you wanted to be promoted, you needed to show you could discipline someone beneath you in rank to prove your power and strength of personality. How can any uniform, detachment or unit manager try to think outside the box when the "brass" will drown you if you do not follow their lead? Therein lies the biggest problem. It is as simple as the schoolyard bully. Unfortunately, I could not find one single manager to stand up to the system, to the bullies. They would empathize with me and feel bad, then watch me suffer, relapse and almost succumb to suicide.

Just because you have rank and so-called promoted success does not mean you are perfect at everything or, in some cases, at anything. When a bully or a power-hungry executive rules with an iron fist, demanding all others beneath them to fall in line, and they all do, the little 'fishies' in the pond are finished.

As a constable, I have very limited striking power. I had no one backing me up as they were all afraid. Our Ontario Provincial Police Association (OPPA) was so busy that they too, surprisingly, could not stand tall enough behind me. I stood up to those managers; I even cried and hyperventilated in their offices, telling them what their lack of action was causing me. They did not care a bit. Manager after manager just followed "the book" of policies and procedures.

I will always be a proud member of the OPP. The OPP has been a part of my whole life. I remember the Force in my dad's era, in the era I started in and in today's era. Our uniforms have evolved, along with our cars, use of force options, GPS/Satellite, technology, demographics, societal values, culture, and the list goes on and on. The one area that has stayed still is our Human Resources policies, our dinosaur-attitude style of management and ignorance to see the human behind the badge. I remember many of the OPP slogans over the years, but one stands out above them all in utter failure. That slogan was, "Times Change, and we Change with Them".

Malfunction of
My Main Processor

———◆•◆———

I t is my experience that every person's make-up is partially made up of
life experiences. It does not matter whether you are a first responder or
a baker; what you experience, good and bad, has a part in shaping who
you are or may become. A police officer, in my case, is no different. I have
experienced personal loss, rejections, happiness, anger, frustrations and so
on, and some of these events are now a part of what I perceive and believe.
How I view certain people, events, and how I feel, have been influenced
in some part by simply living life. I feel I need to preface this chapter with
my previous statement. I have no medical or professional accreditation
in the topics I discuss. I am simply a mentally screwed-up cop trying to
understand what has happened to me, and these are those thoughts. So, if
we all grow in some parts based on our experiences in life right from birth,
through childhood, and high school, and into adulthood, it would be
likely that trauma has been part of that journey in one degree or another. I
meet with and have great conversations with other people who suffer from
PTSD, and not all of them are military and first responders. Some people
have experienced extreme trauma at the hands of loved ones, circumstance,
lifestyle, decisions, both good and bad, as well as addiction, isolation and
self-harm. I feel that those traumas have impacted them just as much as
my traumas; the only difference being that almost all of my traumas have
been experienced as a result of my employment as a police officer. I had no
idea just how much each and every experience was changing, altering and

injuring my brain. So, whether I did not know the damage it was causing, and even when I wondered if it was, I was told to suck-it-up. The years of untreated and multiple traumas created such a mess that I felt totally unrepairable. It was so bad, I wanted to, no, I felt I needed to, end my life. Suicide used to baffle me, but now after living my life, I now know that while it is described as selfish, it is simply a person needing the pain to stop, with no other plausible solution visible to them at that moment.

I have no appetite for getting into each and every traumatic event, as a traumatic event can be interpreted, defined and experienced differently by each person. What I will say is that as a police officer, I experienced what some doctors have described as cumulative traumas over a long period of time. I will say that I have pointed my gun at someone and issued the police challenge and have had a gun pointed towards me. I have investigated homicides, suicides and sudden deaths, some of which are burned into my mind. I have been dispatched to fatal and personal injury collisions, some more tragic and gruesome than the next. I have notified parents, spouses and children of deaths in their family as well as investigated sexual assaults and even acts against the mentally disabled. I have pulled the body of a drowning victim out of a river while the family watched from the shore. I have been in trouble and needed to activate my emergency button asking for backup right away, as well as responded to assist a fellow officer under the same circumstances. I have been in high-speed pursuits and crashes and attended countless post mortems (autopsies), and watched the pathologists do their thing. I have laughed, I have been angry, and I have cried. The calls go on and on.

Now I at least understand where my brain injury came from, but how did my entire life get affected? My brain literally began to change how I reacted to all events, at work, at home or even during leisure activities. How I perceived a situation, acted and spoke were all different than before. It was as if for a moment in time, I was not me. PTSD has stolen from me, as well from my family. I began to live a life on the edge, 24/7. I was constantly in a vigilant state, ready to explode into action. Unfortunately, I use the term 'explode' on purpose. I am married with 2 children; they were unwilling participants in these fits. I have always been a fun and happy-go-lucky guy. Now I became a beast at home. The smallest thing would become of great importance and failure during my processing. My reaction would be an angry outburst, that would confuse and stun my family. I, on the other hand, was beside myself in anger, not being able to rationalize why they did not get it; why they had the nerve to tell me it was time for supper while I was busy. I will focus an entire chapter on the family dynamic, as it is such a crucial topic and experience that needs to be shared.

I am a fairly big man, 5'10" and at the time, about 270 lbs. While I cannot say it was all pure muscle, I could handle my own and generally was not fearful day to day for my safety. That all of a sudden began to change. I could not handle being out in public, especially large stores or events. I would constantly scan everyone around me, looking for their hands, watching for signs of gang or group activity that may be dangerous. I wanted to see in every direction. My mind was focused and preoccupied ALL the time. Now imagine the scenario I describe above is simply at a mall with your family. I would not engage in conversations with them; I was busy. We had to walk tight along the wall; there was no crazy going from store to store, crossing the hallway without a clear intersection first. If the crowd grew to a point where I could not manoeuvre in a manner I deemed safe, I would put my back against the wall and freeze, often closing my eyes, in a state of pure panic. What really scared me was the fight or flight response. I was afraid I would act inappropriately and simply barge my way out to a place I deemed safe. My confused and always loving wife could only stand there, wondering what was going on.

As this progressed, I started to isolate myself and stay at home at all times. The only time I would go out was if my wife, Kathy, was with me. There were times when I would actually hold the back of her coat or pants and walk behind her to prevent a panic episode. She is 7 inches shorter than me. Can you imagine what must be going through her mind? Before long, even that started to change because I started using and needing alcohol to cope. I would stay at home and drink. If I was alone, it was easy; if people were home, I hid bottles around the house and snuck drinks. I am the primary driver in our house, so when Kathy wanted to go out or even run errands, I would make excuses not to go, or erupt in frustration, because I knew how much I was drinking. Addiction became part of my story and part of my life now.

Sleeping became something that I began to dread. I would experience night terrors. I describe the night terrors as a 3D nightmare. I would re-live actual events, or to spice things up, my mind would create even scarier policing scenarios. I would swing, kick, scream and become terrified. I have damaged a lamp and a couple of clocks as well. I have inadvertently struck my unaware and sleeping wife, luckily never hard or direct, but enough that she was sleeping with one eye open for a time. I often laid there awake, afraid of sleep, so I would move to the couch, so everyone was safe. I absolutely hated myself because of these events. Imagine being a police officer and a confident man, needing guidance from his wife to leave the house if at all, and being afraid to sleep. My triggers, symptoms, and hyper-vigilance were taking over my life, and I was scared, really scared. If I heard a child in a park screaming with laughter or crying from a fall, I could barely handle it. A child's voice was crippling me. I can recall another incident being in a local store that was quite large, so the employees used hand radios to communicate with each other. The squelch of the radio sent me into a panic, and I ran out of the store, once again leaving my wife alone to wonder what the hell happened.

My life was spiralling; my family sat scared and confused all because of an injury to my brain, as a result of the cumulative traumas I was experiencing at work. I could not quit because I had the salary, the benefits, and the pension and I could not ask for help because I was afraid I would be shamed, ignored and ostracized. I have seen it happen to others, and it has happened to me as well. What a position to sit in, in silence. Along with countless others with PTSD, I had to navigate an impossible system with a damaged brain resulting in new and bizarre thought processes and reactions, and just for fun, let's add alcohol.

Alcohol - Seeking to Numb

———◆●◆———

I cannot pinpoint when alcohol became an addiction of necessity. The more I try to think about it, the more confused I get. I mean, I had moments in high school, college, and early adulthood where having a drink or two was very simple to do. During those time periods, like a lot of people, I also got blackout drunk at a party or celebration. Does that define alcoholism? I really believe, in my case, that I define my addiction to alcohol as needing it and not wanting it. So, if I go with that, I would say sometime around 1998 to 2000, while living and working in Hearst, Ontario, my drinking flipped to an addiction. Having said that, I could also include a bunch of drunk episodes before that, mostly with co-workers, yet I still felt in control of deciding to drink or to stop. So, what was the difference – what marked the transition to addiction? There is the million-dollar question. A switch went off – it became a need to drink, or at least get a buzz, if not totally wasted, to live each day.

Certain events in Hearst began to pile on from my experiences in Parry Sound. I started to feel the weight of my mind. I started noticing that I thought of, and dreamt about, what was happening at work. I then had to balance that with a new, young family; our daughter was born in March of 1997. I started looking at some events through her eyes and the 'what if's' played on my mind. So, it was in Hearst, about a year after my little girl was born, that I started to notice that alcohol could settle me down, bring peace to a confused mind. At this same time, my very intuitive wife also noticed that alcohol became more present. She talked to me about it, and of course, I downplayed it all. I told her I was young, had a great group of friends, co-workers, and various sports where having a few drinks was normal. At times I would even get angry and tell her to mind her business, that I earned a few drinks, and I was not the only one and to stop overreacting. Of course, she was not wrong at all. As I continued to drink, she became more concerned and was not afraid to talk to me about it. Kathy was saving me as early as back then. Without even knowing it, she kept triggering my conscience, making me think of what was beginning. Her discussions had me contact our Employee Assistance Program for confidential counselling with a social worker to see if anything was going on. At this point, I still felt very ashamed and afraid of what was going on in my brain. I could see my co-workers around me and thought I was the only one feeling what I was feeling. Because I was posted in Hearst, in Northern Ontario, on page two of the map, there were no social workers within our program. The closest one was in Kapuskasing, an hour's drive each way. There was a six-session limit. I went to four of them, I believe. The conversations were good, and I was able to speak my mind to some degree, but back then, I had no idea just how deep the caverns were that I had dug into my subconscious. While I won't disclose these types of conversations, needless to say, I stopped going knowing that being a police officer was my job and that it supported my family. I either quit my job with a young family to support, or see about some antidepressants with my medical doctor and soldier on. I went to my doctor and was given a low-dose antidepressant, all fixed.

Having done what I thought I should do, I found I was still in trouble. Still dreaming of some nasty events, triggering in public with bouts of anxiety and hyper-vigilance. The alcohol was calming that. The social worker, the antidepressants and self-talk were not. Kathy continued to be eagle-eyed as she still felt my alcohol consumption was too high. Alcohol was the only thing that was working, and now I was looking at Kathy as a threat to losing that as well. So, I did the most reasonable thing I came up with at the time; I started to hide, lie and drink in secret. As the story goes on, that was not a great idea. I guess I figured that as long as I did not let it affect my young family, meaning being drunk and useless, but drunk and useful, she did not need to know. As time progressed, I would still drink socially around her while adding to the drink total in private. I would get caught from time to time; I would make promises, keep breaking them and keep trying to keep the sickness in my mind away. The drink became my equalizer to a happy family, so lying to her was for her, so even though she would be upset with me from time to time, I had all the self-validation I needed to keep going.

I was transferred to North Bay in September of 2000. My parents lived there, and Kathy's parents and her entire family lived there. Things would get better. In October of 2000, one month after the transfer, my son was born. The job I was transferred to was in plain clothes as a Regional Detective. I was off the front-line of "the calls," so I was optimistic the demons of sickness in my mind would relax. That, too, did not work out. Still confused about what was going on with me, my drinking continued to escalate. Drinking became easier because we were a travelling 6-officer unit responsible for the entire Northeast Region, primarily focused on property crimes, but were used for basically all major crimes, from murders, drugs, sex offenders to out-law motorcycle gangs. We were a resource, so we were a unit that would swoop in to help out the area crime units, do our thing and move on to the next area where they needed us. As we were doing our thing, from Ottawa to Toronto to Sault Ste Marie, drinking was easy to accomplish. My conscience was at home, and I was travelling the province in plain vehicles, jeans, investigating or at least being a part of very interesting cases, and hanging out with my kinfolk. Oh, was I drinking! After being in this unit for one year, I needed out. I was drinking basically every day, but the problem still remained that the emotions, feelings and confusing memories were getting really bad. My dreams started to become night terrors, actively fighting in my sleep. I would wake up with a lamp down, blankets everywhere and my wife looking at me with fear and a "what the hell" look on her face. The poor girl had to start sleeping with one eye open.

As mentioned earlier, I kept changing positions at work, trying to make the pain stop. I was drinking like crazy now. I would start schemes of buying two cases of beer, one my wife knew of and one she did not know of. That way, when she checked the case and only saw two beers gone, she was happy, but there were also 10 missing from the hidden case. I then started to make my own wine. I was not a real wine drinker, but it was alright; the buzz counted. I made a red wine that basically cost about 3 dollars a bottle. Each batch made about 30 to 35 bottles. Not a great idea. The bottles started going, and Kathy was starting to wonder. After a few batches of wine, I was instructed maybe I should stop making wine. For a while, we kept the corkscrew upstairs, and the wine and my bar were downstairs. I had a downstairs walk-out to my garage. What I started to do was take a bottle of wine, go in the garage, flip a nail upside down, head against the cork and hammer the cork into the bottle. Down it went. It was getting so bad that when we had plans to go out for the evening, I would agree on a certain number of drinks beforehand, but knew that would not work, so I would tell her I would meet her at the car. I was able to grab a bottle of wine, nail the cork out and chug a full bottle of wine all at once. This took me less than 3 minutes, giving me time to compose myself before Kathy could get to the car. One last story about my deceptive tactics. I built a workbench in the garage, and during the construction, I built hidden compartments that could easily and quickly hide a beer, liquor or wine bottle. Tell me that is normal behaviour.

As I bounced around positions with the OPP and continued to battle the flawed Human Resources and accommodation processes, all the while being in so much pain and distress, my life was spiralling out of control. It was November 2011. The North Bay staff-sergeant-of-the-day pulled strings with our very dazed command staff and I returned to the front line, as the community service officer, because the current one had left the detachment. I was finally stabilizing, but back I went. This job involved going to schools to talk about the perils of alcohol, drugs and bullying, as well as attending public events and handling media relations. "It was not front line", they said - wrong. I was out of positions, the OPP were so lost with mental health injuries, I was absolutely cornered. "It was not front line", they said - wrong. I was running out of options. The OPP was so lost with mental health injuries, this seemed like a solution to them, but I was absolutely cornered. I was now drinking every day - finding and hiding money wherever I could. Lying to my family. I was so dazed, confused and angry that my wife and kids avoided me. I would pass out on the couch, eat dinner, and start to get a hangover, so I was in bed by 7:00 or 8:00 PM. Wake up, go to work and repeat. I admitted to my wife that I was an alcoholic and promised to never drink again. Another lie. I then found I needed to hide, plan and scheme even more carefully; I would find the money through cash-back programs and other banking methods. I also worked harder to not get caught drinking. The problem was, when you are a drunk, it is so hard to keep your act together. I would forget conversations, forget where I hid my booze, leave empties in the garbage or blue bin – hell, I had a hard enough time just living; trying to be sneaky was a joke.

What absolutely saved my life was my wife Kathy's love for me, and her devotion and tenacity to help me and not give up on me. I gave up on myself; she would not. She would later tell me that she knew the Shawn she married was still there, and she was going to help me through my battles. She knew I was suffering from Post Traumatic Stress Disorder. She was with me through psychiatric and psychological assessments, and diagnoses. She knew my PTSD was extreme, constantly triggered, and watched as the OPP let me hang out to dry. She worked with my parents, pleaded with the OPP, doctors, and whomever could help me that I needed help. Kathy was scared, and she had every right to be.

In the spring of 2013, Kathy saw an article in our OPPA (Ontario Provincial Police Association) magazine from the wife of an OPP officer who took his own life as a result of PTSD. The officer was around my age, had children, married and even went for some PTSD treatments. When he went back to work, he took his own life. The widow in the article was asking, no, telling all other members to speak up and get the help they need. It was a very gripping article. Well, Kathy read the article and brought the magazine over to me. With tears in her eyes, she said very firmly, "don't you ever do this to me". Of course, I promised I wouldn't, and reached for another drink.

Years after this incident happened, I was reading a subscription that I have from a magazine called Grapevine. Grapevine is a monthly magazine published by the Head Office of Alcoholics Anonymous in New York City, which contains stories from Alcoholics around the world sharing their knowledge, strength and hope in battling alcoholism. This one particular story had the following sentence that is so clear to me today, but was so blurry back then. It said, "If I was angry, lonely, sad or afraid and I drank, I became drunk and angry, drunk and lonely, drunk and sad or drunk and afraid. I had never had good feelings from drinking; I drank because I had to." This remains a profound statement for me today.

In May 2013, my alcoholism, night terrors, triggers, anxiety and hyper-vigilance were completely out of control. I was in so much pain. The alcohol was not working anymore; it was now another problem I had to contend with, along with the PTSD. When I was sober, I was in a constant state of confusion, fear and sadness, but when I was drunk, I was drunk along with a haze of anger and self-hatred. The PTSD, the flawed human resources, WSIB, OPP managers and alcohol abuse had taken their toll. I arrived at work, changed into my uniform, holstered up, went to my office, closed the door and sat at my desk. I sat there for over an hour, crying, absolutely seeing no way out. I had a family that loved me, but I was causing them so much pain, fear and worry. The OPP refused to help me, the WSIB was leading me along a pitiful, punishing journey of failure, and I could not stop drinking. I could not live sober, and now I couldn't seem to live drunk. I never understood what makes a person commit suicide; it used to baffle me. At that very moment I understood. Suicide was not about the selfish act of killing yourself, it was simply an act to stop the pain from which no other plausible outcome could be seen.

I reached into my desk, pulled out two cans of tall boy 'Ice' beer, and chugged each one in one gulp to get the mind a little numb and dazed. I walked into the change-room, went to the tiled part of the room and un-holstered my firearm.

GUNPOINT

—————•————

There is sadness, but this was total bewildered despair. As I recall this very difficult memory of my journey, I can say that I saw no other option that provided my mind with any clarity and peace. Every option I envisioned, every management member of the OPP I turned to, every doctor, every pill, every clone member of the WSIB, and every bottle of alcohol I could consume, were all brick walls. I had no options that, at that moment, were viable to any sort of personal life, let alone a husband and a father. I had love and support within my family. My wife was and still is to this day the biggest rockstar and hero I have. My children and I were close, and I knew they loved me, and they knew that I loved them. My parents were always there. They offered no judgements, just love and an unequivocal passion and devotion to their son. However, I sincerely felt they were better off without my burden as, at that moment, I could not fathom peace; therefore, no one would have peace in my presence, even though it was unintentional. When I speak of this terrible moment, I want to emphasize the phrase "at that moment". A moment in time can be fleeting, and is often quickly replaced by a new moment. It is the gap between moments where the danger of suicide and death is real.

There are so many ways someone can die, either naturally, traffic accident, murder, suicide, etc. I thought of the ways and was quite rational with myself. Without getting all dark, I decided on my service pistol for a few reasons. It was convenient, and hatching a scheme to obtain a firearm was not needed. Our ammunition then were hollow point .40 calibre bullets. They go in with a small hole and come out the other side a much larger hole, ensuring the job gets done the first time and without a mere injury to add to the pile of despair. The final reason was, after the deed, my family would not be able to see me in death, and hopefully the memories of better times would be in their thoughts. How screwed up is that?

After drinking the beer, I headed to the change-room. I did a walkthrough of the shower and locker room portion to ensure no one was in there. The last thing I needed was some hero to stop me, send me to the Psych Hospital, and the shit would keep piling on. Once that area was clear, I moved to the tiled bathroom portion of the room. Empty. I turned my back to the mirror and un-holstered my weapon. The first thing I did was look down the barrel to ensure a round was at the ready. I had just loaded the gun an hour or so earlier, so I knew there was a bullet up the chamber, but I had to be sure. When I saw the hollow point portion of the bullet looking back at me, tears started to roll down my cheeks. I wasn't crying, but tears flowed slowly. I put the gun up against my temple, just above the ear on my right side. I then was unsure if I should keep the barrel straight or turn slightly towards the face or the back of the skull. I brought the gun down and looked at it. I decided to put the gun in my mouth.

I opened my mouth and pointed the barrel inside, slightly knocking my lower teeth. I closed my lips around the barrel, and the tears seemed to be flowing faster. I then noticed the taste of the gun oil; the lubricant we use to maintain the weapon. My finger was on the trigger and I began to put pressure on it. I felt the trigger start moving. It was happening; the moment was now.

I want to draw your attention to a couple of things I mentioned earlier. If you will recall, in early May, Kathy showed me the article written by the widow of an OPP officer who had committed suicide. As the trigger pull was in motion, I had the most angelic, confusing and powerful moment I have ever had. My eyes were open because of the tears, but all I could hear was a hum. With my eyes wide open, my mind showed me the moment Kathy was showing me that article. It was not like a vision; it was like I was watching the moment on a screen. I could see her talking to me. I could see the passion on her face, the magazine in her hand, and the only words I heard her say were, "don't you ever do this to me". I ended the trigger pull and briefly kept the gun in my mouth. The screen was gone, but Kathy's message raged through me. I pulled the gun out of my mouth and holstered it. I turned around to look at the mirror and saw a horrible sight. The tears were not just running slowly down my cheeks, I was soaked, and had snot everywhere; my face looked exhausted. I looked at myself and realized the other point I mentioned a bit earlier; I managed to get through one moment and safely travelled to the next moment in time. This moment was of relief, this moment was powerful and Kathy provided the fuel. I cleaned up my face before someone came in, and then just stared in the mirror. My perspective at that very moment changed. I knew the next step, and it would be very hard on me.

The staff sergeant's office was right behind the door to the change room. He was one of the managers that ignored mental illness and impeded any progress my doctors and I were trying to make. He forced me back to the uniform, and his attitude allowed me to justify my drinking and downward spiral. I now had to face him if I was to get any sort of help. I needed to walk through that door. My eyes were swollen, and my heart was beating so fast. I needed to ask for help, swallow my pride, my ego, and my morals of what is right and wrong. I paused, then flung the change room door open, and walked right into the staff sergeant's office. I did not ask, I did not knock, I just walked right in, shut the door behind me. I was in for a pleasant surprise.

I turned around and faced the man behind the desk. I was stunned at who was sitting in the chair. He looked at me and said, "Hi Six Pack, what's up?" It was Sergeant Dean Ward. The usual staff sergeant was away, so Sergeant Ward was the acting detachment commander at this present time. Sergeant Ward was a friend, and one of the very few supervisors that cared for the members under his command. He wanted to know how everyone was doing, not just while working. He had an interest in us, our families and our well-being. He treated every member like this. He has a very upbeat personality, and was the exact person I needed behind that chair at that moment. I was so vulnerable and anxious, but seeing his smiling face, allowed me to relax and let go.

Before I carry on, I should address why Sergeant Ward referred to me as "Six Pack" when he said hello. Sergeant Ward was the sergeant in command of the crime team that I travelled the province with, as I mentioned earlier. Back then, in 2000, we were called the Rural and Agricultural Crime Team (RACT), but today this team of detectives is called the Regional Support Team (RST). Usually, when you are a part of such a crime team, especially when you conduct surveillance and undercover work, you have a nickname or a "handle." The team refers to one another, especially over the radio and phone, with their handle instead of their real name so that people with scanners and such do not know your identity. This helps protect the officers and prevents the "target," who may be listening, from knowing which unit we belong to. Here's the thing, you are not allowed to pick your own handle; the members of the team do. Once a nickname is chosen, it sticks for the rest of your career, carrying over to any unit or team you may belong to going forward, as well. I have come to like my handle, but the story behind how I got it is not that glamorous.

I would love to tell you that the handle Six Pack refers to my level of fitness and washboard abs, but sadly, it does not. Maybe a couple or three decades ago, but not so much now. There was a competition when this Crime Team was formed in September 2000. Officers from across the region applied. They selected a team leader, which was Sergeant Ward and 5 detective constables; I was one of the selected detectives. Before the team went operational in the field, we attended training courses together, such as break and enter investigations and a lot of mobile (vehicle and on foot) surveillance. It was intense and a lot to learn, but a great way to get to know your new team, and build a bond and trust. Sergeant Ward and one of the other detectives already had their handle from previous units, so that left four of us to be named.

I was first, and it came with a great deal of ribbing. The first course we went on together actually occurred at our general headquarters in Orillia, even before any of us were transferred to North Bay. I was working in Hearst, so I had to travel the 8 hours or so to attend. We all travelled in from across the North East and met at the hotel booked for us to stay. I only really knew Sergeant Ward. I knew a few other officers but did not know much about them. Before we travelled down, one of the guys assigned who would bring what. They told one guy to bring snacks and such, and I was assigned to buy the beer for everyone. I honestly did not think they were serious; as a young officer with a toddler and an 8-month pregnant wife both at home, money was not really all that flush. I never thought they were serious about buying beer for 6 guys. Turns out it was, in fact, just a joke, but what I did when I arrived at the hotel was the solidifying moment of Six Pack. I met my new team in someone's hotel room and walked through the door with a six-pack of beer. It took just one guy to immediately say, "What the hell is with a six-pack? You only brought one each?" They all started jumping on board and laughing. I, of course, was the youngest guy in the room, and I was stammering along trying to justify my six-pack and thought it was just a joke. I cannot remember exactly who said it first, but within 45 seconds of walking in that hotel room, they shouted out, "Hey that's it, his handle should be Six Pack." They all agreed, and so it was decreed. Six Pack was my handle.

When I looked into the Sergeant's eyes, I sat down and let it all out. Well, almost all of it. I simply said, "Dean I need your help." He made some phone calls and brought me to his house; no one from his family was home. He did this so other people would not see me or overhear what was happening. He then arranged to have 2 members of our Critical Incident Support team come to his house. I told them that I was diagnosed with PTSD and that I am now an alcoholic who cannot stop drinking. I told them I was depressed and overwhelmed and needed to stop. I did not however, at that time, mention I drank at my desk, nor did I tell them about my gun. You see, even when I was letting go and being vulnerable, I still could not let it all out; those barriers of trust were still rather thick. I also figured they would take my gun and use of force belt, and ship me to a Psych hospital. I knew how that worked. They helped organize a plan through our association (OPPA) and my medical doctor. Within a few days, I was a resident of a 5-week program at the Homewood Health Centre for treatment of alcohol addiction and attending a Uniform Members Trauma group and a society-based Trauma group. Day one was June 5th, 2013.

As an interesting side note, I should explain my last day of work and my escorted trip to Homewood. If you recall, my current duties were that of the Community Services Officers. As part of those duties, I taught grade 5 and 6 students Drug Abuse Resistance Education (DARE). I taught in well over 10 schools around our Detachment area. By the end of May, most course classes are completed, and the last week of May, the start of June, is when I have the DARE graduations at each school. It was a big event with members of the DARE board, OPP Officer Managers. When the suit was available, even Darren, our lion mascot, would be there. You can imagine the emotional toll it took on me to warn and teach students about the dangers of drugs and alcohol while abusing the shit out of alcohol daily. I had such a poor attitude about myself for a lot of reasons, but this was very hard. I needed to be the upbeat "Constable Shawn" in the classroom, and then the lying, cheating and hiding alcoholic when off-duty. I really wanted to make sure all of my students received their graduation before I was sent away. They earned it; it really chipped away at my very core. So, it was decided, I would be driven down to Guelph, Ontario, where the Homewood Treatment Centre is, on June 4th, 2013. I would stay in a hotel overnight and then be admitted at 9 am on June 5th, 2013.

The morning of June 4th, I was decked out in my #1 Dress Uniform as I always did for my final DARE graduation. It was a grand ceremony. At noon, I was at home getting out of my uniform and putting on street clothes. At around 1 pm, I was picked up by a sergeant of the Crisis Incident Team and driven to Guelph. Irony, sadness, guilt and shame, all in the same day.

Homewood Treatment Centre

At 9 AM a taxi dropped me off at the front entrance to Homewood Treatment Centre. The driver unloaded my suitcase and left. I stood looking at the steps to the front entrance. Until this very moment, I did not realize exactly where I was going. Suddenly, it hit me that I was about to enter rehab and that my life was out of my control.

I walked to the front information desk to tell them the glorious news that I was here to check-in. I was directed to a door just down the hall and wheeled my suitcase over to it. Over the next 5 weeks, I would see many people, just like me, make that short walk to the registration door with luggage in tow. Most had the same look I had that day; what the hell happened?

Once inside, I sat in a small waiting room, gripping my bag and contemplating running away. I mean literally running away. My name was called, and I was directed to an office, my suitcase was taken, and I was told I would see it later. I registered and signed a whole bunch of documents, and to this day, I cannot tell you what most of them were. I knew they were insurance-based and the like, but I was still in total disbelief. I was a police officer, a husband, and a dad; why am I being admitted? My head was in a dizzying trance. I kept telling myself that I needed help to keep my family, job and sanity. I went into a robotic and compliant state. After I signed some papers, I was introduced to an older man who was a volunteer at the centre. He was going to escort me to the area of the centre where I would be staying. I simply followed.

I was escorted to my room. It had 2 single beds, 2 closets and 2 end tables. It was obvious I had a roommate, but he wasn't in the room. I sat there looking around. Instead of being sad, I was quite angry with myself. I felt that I was so weak that I needed rehab and counselling. I would soon learn just how far from the truth my feelings were at that time. A nurse came into the room and went over a few housekeeping rules. They confiscated my CPAP machine, used for sleep apnea, to inspect it and ensure it met their electrical systems standards. My CPAP machine? She advised I would get it back before bed and seized all of my prescription drugs, explaining they would administer them to me each morning. So, I even lost control over my blood pressure and brain-candy drugs. Do you want to know how they administer them to you? A nurse does not bring you your pills and a cup of water at the bedside. Oh no. Every morning I had to stand in line with the other 100 or so patients down the hallway. This was done every morning and every evening. Thankfully, my meds were only taken in the morning, so it was only one line-up for me. Once my turn had come, they handed me my meds, and I had to consume them right there in front of them. Some people, depending on their meds, had to show a clear mouth afterwards, too. I guess my drugs were not required for such measures.

The nurse left with my meds and CPAP machine, and she advised that my assigned nurse would be by shortly for my admission interview. As I waited, my roommate walked in. For the love of God. He was in his 50's but dressed like Vanilla Ice with his baggy sports gear, runners and backwards ball cap. He introduced himself and then started to talk, and talk, and would not shut up. He asked what I did for a living and what chemical got me in this place. I lied and told him I worked for Hydro and was here to deal with alcohol issues. Thankfully my nurse walked in and told my roommate to get to his next class before he was late.

She was a very nice nurse and seemed to genuinely be interested in my journey and recovery. We went over my physical health history and then discussed my mental health. She had most of my mental health assessment files, so she had a general idea of the state of my PTSD and alcoholism. We stayed together for a couple of hours, and for that time, I felt that perhaps I would benefit from this in-patient facility. She explained the house rules, including what infractions warranted immediate removal from Homewood. There were to be no relationships at all. You were not allowed to have anyone from the opposite sex in your room, period. Angry outbursts and any violence at all would send you packing, and then likely relapsing. I was told I was assigned to a certain group, about 25 or so residents, and that would be my group for the duration of my stay. Each group had a medical doctor, a counsellor, social worker and a fitness associate. Our group also had a student psychologist, doing his placement for his licence, I suppose. I would meet with every one of these professionals and my entire group every morning for a round circle they called "Pots and Pans."

Pots and Pans was when all the residents would identify themselves, their addiction and sober or clean date, along with one word or so to describe how they are feeling at that moment. They did however, ban the emotions of happy, sad and mad. The emotion needed to be deeper than that. For example, every morning for 5 weeks, I would say, "My name is Shawn, and I am an alcoholic; I have been sober since June 5th" (2013). The very first time, I described my emotion as confused. This time is also used for our recovery team to keep us up-to-date on what was going on with our progress, or provide changes to our scheduled treatments based on our progression in the program. More on that later. It was also a chance that if you needed to speak with the doctor or anyone else on the team you could ask them, and vice versa, if they wanted to meet with you.

The other daily occurrence was something similar to Pots and Pans, but it happened every night at 8 pm, with the same assigned group. However, this session was led by one of the nurses. We had to do the same introduction; addiction and sober date and how we were feeling at that time. We sat at a round table and discussed how people were feeling, or what issues they were dealing with. These were not the regular treatment sessions, they were just a nightly touch base. After that, we had free-time until 11 pm, at which time it was a mandatory lights out.

Thankfully my roommate was not in my recovery group, or I would have been thrown out for losing my cool. So, my first night at rehab was spent with a jacked-up squirrel, who clearly had no ability to shut up, have a regular conversation or enjoy sleep. He went on and on. I even told him to stop talking, then put on my CPAP mask, turned it on and rolled away from him to face the wall, and he still would not shut up. The next morning, squirrelly boy was chatting up a freaking storm again. I was so happy he was not in my recovery group. Before we left for breakfast or Pots and Pans, a nurse came to our room and advised me that I would need to go for the introduction blood and urine test on the first floor. A baseline, I suppose. My very next question made it so that the rapid-repeater had to escort me down. All I asked the nurse was, where can I find this lab? Megamouth jumped up and volunteered to escort me so I would not get lost. The nurse thought it was a good idea. Mother of God.

My first few days at Homewood were quite uneventful. I went to their programming classes and basically got myself adjusted to being there. I was admitted on a Thursday and did not have enough time to earn privileges yet, which meant I had to stay the weekend on the property. The weekend was quiet, with fewer residents and administration staff. It was basically the nurses running the show. I must say, throughout my stay, the nurses were amazing. They seemed like they cared for all of us, as well, they would set you straight if you dared push your luck. I like that kind of leadership. If you work hard, and play within the rules, you were treated fairly, but if you fuck about, you were going to have to answer for your behaviour. It kind of ran along the "honest pay for an honest day's work" expression. I was fortunate that my skilled auctioneer roommate had a weekend pass. I was able to meet a lot of people and tour the vast building and property.

Let me tell you about some of the residents. There were medical and psychiatric doctors, nurses, military personnel, engineers, construction workers, transit drivers and even the odd "law-abiding challenged" individual. There was every walk of life in there, all genders, lifestyles and occupations. I learned from every single one of them. What I appreciated the most about Homewood was that I was referred to as Shawn, and not Constable Fougère of the OPP. Actually, no one really cared about what you "did" or how you identified yourself. We were all there for the same reason: to get better. I still have many friends from my time there.

After another rough Sunday night when my chatty roommate returned from his weekend, I could not see myself lasting. I went to the nurse's station and begged for a different room and roommate change. I explained my lack of sleep, lack of judgement processing and my anger issues as a result of my mental health condition. I was moved that afternoon. What a relief!

I appreciated that at Homewood; everyone was there for the same reason. The substance of addiction might vary, but the disease was the same. No one was better than anyone; no one was any worse. Once I was comfortable, I could topple all the walls I had built up during my 42-year life. However, I fought the feeling for the first week. When I met my group doctor during my admission interview, we went through my history, especially my drinking history, to ascertain if I required medical assistance during the beginning of abstinence. He was a great doctor, and he made me feel comfortable, so I first opened up to him at about 80% honesty. I was not his first resident intake interview, and he knew my walls and that the whole truth around my drinking shenanigans was not being told. He concluded his assessment by ordering that I receive a vitamin B shot in the ass, to give my system some assistance during early admission. Pants down, needle to the cheek. What a day.

During that first discovery week, I was also put in my place by the staff there. Like I said, they put up with nothing. Your recovery and health were their only concern, not your bullshit. We had to attend Alcoholic Anonymous (AA) meetings daily. I had attended the "closed" AA meeting in the past, but I was fairly new to these meetings. The closed meeting is, generally, for alcoholics, or people who feel they may be, and want to stop drinking. At these meetings, a person or persons stood at the front of the room and told their story or their journey. They basically tell you what it was like during active addiction, how they found and worked recovery, and how their life is today. On day 3 or 4, our group counsellor advised us that there would be 2 people speaking that night who were relatively new to the program, and would be sharing their stories. So that evening, I went down to the theatre type hall at Homewood, and these 2 guys were introduced. They had no public speaking skills and were very hard to follow. I soon became disinterested and allowed my mind to wander.

The next morning, during our group session, the counsellor asked what we thought of the speakers at the meeting last night. No one spoke up, so she volunteered me and asked what I learned from the speakers. Without hesitation, I said, "not a thing, they were hard to listen to." She straightened up in her chair and told me in a very stern and elevated voice to "Get Out." Pardon? "Get out. I will be out to see you shortly." Very red in the face, with 25 or so others staring at me, I got up and walked out into the hallway and stood there. Now, when I was in elementary school, I will admit my jocularity in class did cause me to spend some time in the hallway, but now I was a 42-year-old man, and I was back in the hallway. Within a few minutes, she came out to see me. She looked me square in the eye and said one of the best things I could have heard that early on. I am paraphrasing, but her message was to drop the ego and listen to everyone who shares their story. Everyone has a story worth sharing. If I chose to listen, I may hear something that I did not know before and it may contribute to my recovery. She also said that those men were new and probably really nervous, and shame on me for criticizing their presentation skills and missing the entire point of recovery. She escorted me back into the room, and I sat down. With that, I got to work.

At around the second-week mark, I began specific recovery groups focused on trauma. While my primary program was alcohol addiction, I attended a trauma group, which consisted of anyone who had experienced trauma. I also participated in a Uniform Trauma group intended for police and military members. The first group I went to was the Uniform Trauma group. There were 6 of us in the group initially, but it fluctuated with new admissions and releases. The sessions were led by a psychologist. She guided the talks and made sure discussions stayed on point. While I will not identify any of the stories or agencies out of respect for privacy, I can tell you this group opened me up. I had a skeptical attitude about "group" anything. I did not like group work in school, training, or anything. I was a lone wolf. In the first session, I mostly listened to the others. My jaw kept getting wider and wider. These people were expressing exactly how I was feeling. I understood exactly how they explained things. The whole group nodded their heads, and the psychologist knew how to keep things progressing in a comfortable manner. Some of the things we spoke of were horrific, but in this room, I felt like I could talk about anything I experienced because they understood the context; they understood the career and life of the profession.

One military person in the group had been there longer than I had. This person had already begun to clear away some of the emotions and scars in a more tolerable and acceptable manner. What I mean is that this person was able to articulate their experiences and emotions matter-of-factly for discussion. During the second session, my band-aid was ripped right off, and what came out was anger, resentment, and the feeling of abandonment by the OPP. As I relayed some of my experiences, my teeth would grit, spit would fly, and I was on the edge. The psychologist also worked with me, so she knew where I was emotionally. She gave me latitude, but her eyes could speak and reminded me to stay connected. After the first time I spoke up in this manner, that military employee I spoke of piped up and said, "I thought I had anger, but you are one angry man." That statement from this person really opened my mind about where I needed to start this recovery journey.

The Trauma group I belonged to included a larger group of people, about 10 to 15, at any given time. It was mentored by the same psychologist as the Uniformed Trauma group. In this group, I discovered that PTSD is not specific to just police, military or first responders. PTSD is a diagnosis for anyone. In this group, I learned recovery and trigger techniques used by non-police people in their recovery. This was important because sometimes, even in suffering and recovery, the police bravado can get in the way. If you are always speaking to the same type of people, in the same field of exposure, you run the risk of adapting, or even trying to fit other people's trauma into your own, instead of just the action of mental health symptoms. If you are always speaking to the same type of people, in the same field of exposure, you run the risk of adapting, or even absorbing, other people's trauma into your own. In my experience, for the recovery process to be productive, you must be authentic and focused on your personal story and symptoms. The incidents or the stories inflicted may be at the root of trauma, but trying to deal with the symptoms while living day-to-day is what helps me the most. When I have the opportunity in treatment, whether through one-on-one sessions or within a group, I find it more practical to discuss the suffering emotions, such as fear, anger, isolation, hyper-vigilance, etc., and techniques to overcome those states of mind to lessen their disturbance to my day-to-day life. I do not enjoy sharing war stories; we all have them.

During my stay at Homewood, I participated in every recommended activity and session. I did the assigned homework, which were excellent exercises in self-reflection. I am very happy that the stiff upper lip I wore when I walked in that door only lasted a few days. You need to put in the work. If my rockstar group staff team taught me anything, it was that.

Learn the techniques, keep an open mind and do the work. That was a very easy sentence to write, but really hard to do sometimes.

Throughout my stay, I had a total of four roommates. Two of them identified as drug addicts and two as alcoholics. Recovery, conversations and group discussions did not differentiate between the drug of your addiction. One of the activities they offered, and that I participated in, was a gardening-type class. We pruned and transplant shrubs and learned different gardening techniques. I painted a western steer skull in a pottery class. I made bracelets and bookmarks out of raw leather. I also bowled and played board games. Each activity was guided, and in reflection, each one had a purpose, I just needed to keep my mind open. I did have my moments, I can assure you, where I wanted to run for the hills. I was sleeping in a small room with another addict, had a bedtime, a full scheduled day of requirements, and just like our police guards check on the prisoners in their cells, the nurses came around in the middle of the night with their flashlights to do bed checks. I witnessed some moments where a resident or residents were kicked out for breaking the no-no rules. There was also some conflict between people, but my goal was to work on myself. Whether right or wrong, I did not worry about anyone else in there. I did not get involved in any outside issues, and I did not get too attached to people, I just kept myself busy.

The other emotional drain being at a treatment centre was my family members at home. Kathy was able to rationalize, understand, and was grateful I was getting help. My kids, on the other hand, were another issue to me personally. Kathy and I sat them down and told them a lot of the truths, and of course, they could also see for themselves that daddy needed some help. They handled it well, but it killed me. My son was in grade 7, and my daughter in grade 10. I was a very active member of the community and the kids' activities, so questions would definitely be asked as to where I was. We developed a group story that I had gone away for work training. I had been away a lot before, and for long periods because of training, so the story worked seamlessly.

Asking for help and acknowledging to yourself and others that you are having mental issues and /or addiction issues is horribly painful. I will never say it is easy. I was afraid some of my coworkers would turn their backs on me. Sadly a lot of them did. I was also scared management would black ball me, and they did. I was worried about how the community and my kids would react. There are a lot of thoughts going through your mind when you feel like there are no options. I can recall that feeling like it was yesterday. Everything and everyone in my life appeared to have taken a toll and I felt like I could not recover. When I thought of solutions, I did not see any. My go-to response, being alcohol, was fuelling that hollow feeling even more. I am very proud and very grateful that I holstered my weapon that day. I am so thankful to my wife, Kathy, for showing me that article and telling me she was going to be there for me. She planted the seed that I was able to recall at that pivotal moment. While I still have struggles with my PTSD and some alcohol relapses, I am alive to see everything I am grateful for. I still attend monthly meetings with my psychologist and appointments with my medical doctor every 3 months. I am involved in a 12-step recovery program and have been blessed to have met people like me, and made great friendships. Before asking for help, I almost ended my life, like, sadly, quite a few others have before me. This is the reason I am sharing my story. Trust at least one person and choose life. I have heard this quote many times before, and now that my mind is clearer, I believe it to be true. "Do not do something permanent to solve a temporary problem." I look back at over 10 years of pain and addiction, and while I was blinded then, my eyesight is returning. For that I am forever in debt to Kathy, Sergeant Dean Ward and, of course, to my own strength. This strength is in all of us.

On July 11th, 2013, I was released from Homewood Treatment Centre with a new sense of hope, coping strategies and the feeling of being on a pink cloud. Now back to life.

THE FAMILY DYNAMIC

———— ◆•◆ ————

B efore I share what life was like once released from Homewood Treatment Centre, I would like to talk about how my demons, illnesses and addictions affected my family. Like many other families in similar situations, alcoholism, addictions and illnesses bring family members along for the ride, even if the addict does not recognize it. I felt for years that my alcohol consumption did not affect my family because I was only hurting myself. Was I ever wrong!

I have been blessed in recovery to speak to different groups on the effects of mental illness, in particular, Post Traumatic Stress Disorder injury. I am an open book and honest speaker who tells it like it was for me. I will discuss this a bit later in the book in more detail, but there was one particular speaking engagement in front of 300 + people from across Canada and a few delegates from the United States. Before the event, they asked me to send them a picture and a brief summary of my topic presentation to include in their program. While constructing this summary, the toll my illnesses and addictions had on my family hit me over the head like a hammer. What was more surprising about my astonishment at the words was the very fact I wrote them. Here is an excerpt of that bio;

> *"Shawn Fougère, Police Officer, Father, Husband*
> *and Fighter, and Kal, Service Dog - Shawn is a*
> *25-year veteran police officer who is also a human*
> *being struggling through mental illness injuries and*

> *addiction. He has served the public, from investigating homicides to fender benders, while guiding both he and his family through a dark and grim journey of self-destruction, self medication, eventually resulting in a gun point all-or-nothing decision."*

The bio continues, but the opening is still one of the best collection of words I can use to describe the feelings of my journey so far. Every footstep, conversation, melt down, drunk, rage-induced confusion, and experiences of day-to-day living I have had since this shit show started, has been taken with my wife and children right beside me. I wish I would have rationalized this statement earlier on to myself because the disease, the illness and my behaviour, as a result, has hurt them deeply and changed them forever. There are a lot of people who would do anything to keep their family safe, happy and healthy. I am one of those people. I would give my life for theirs' in a heartbeat. As a police officer, I even agreed to give my life for people I did not know because that is the person I am. Then why did I not see my wife and children beside me for so long? How did I not realize that my continual triggers, anxiety, panic, depression, anger, sadness and extreme isolation episodes were witnessed and shared by them? How did I not see that my diagnosis and treatment options of PTSD, substance abuse and addictions would not affect them? I even thought during my suicide attempt, that I was doing them a favour! My untreated mental health injury and all of its apostles of despair were causing my family to twirl in confusion and disarray.

This is my story and my answers to my behaviour. I did not realize the toll my health issues had on my family initially because I thought I was keeping it a really big secret. I was burying everything deep down inside to avoid hurting them. I was drinking in secret so that they would not see an alcoholic husband or father. I could probably write a book simply with my excuses, lies and rationalization that I used for so many years. I thought I was protecting them. I was wrong, and it almost killed me, destroyed our family and it has changed our lives forever. By the grace of God, I had that moment of clarity in the change room. My life and the lives of my family had begun to heal and improve once I realized I needed to talk and say the hardest word in the English language for me - Help!

One of my big roadblocks to honesty and saying the H-word was my belief in stigma. Stigma to me means the reaction of employers, managers, friends, family, and even the general public, that cause me to feel weak, ashamed, alone and a disgrace because of my feelings (illness). As much as I was worried about the reactions from work, I also feared these same feelings from my family. I convinced myself that my wife and kids would think less of me if I said the H-word. Stigma is evil and can be fatal. This applies to anyone fearful of what others may think. You do not have to be a police officer to feel shame about a mental illness. I see it way too often. My family is still with me today, and they have battled with me every day. For that I am experiencing life after the change-room. It was finally putting my hands up and gun down and saying, "help!" that started to heal us all. I cannot say this enough: to anyone who is living the pain like I was in that change-room, please choose life. Just trust one person.

Today, I am free from stigma. I am no longer ashamed. I would never compare a mental health illness to, let's say, cancer, just as I could not compare an apple to an orange; however they are both fruit! I have been a member of the OPP family since May 1992 and I have donated money frequently, whether through BBQ's, T-shirt sales, GoFundMe pages etc., supporting fellow employees suffering a physical illness or injury, but no one has even thought of the financial struggles for someone like me! Mental illness has not been seen in the same way as other illnesses. Why? Perception, ignorance and stigma. Due to my illness, my income was affected, and I struggled to make ends meet. I needed to travel, stay in hotels and pay for meals while training with my service dog and receiving treatments. I racked up a credit card to $7000.00, which has taken Kathy and me a few years to pay off. I am not mentioning this as a sob story but simply describing the inherent negative bias towards mental health illness and injuries.

A mental health diagnosis can occur over time, genetically, if you will. There can also be an event or events that create the illness, the exact same way as any other physical illness or disease. They both cause pain, stress, worry, financial hardship, and they both can kill you.

While I thought I was so sneaky and not affecting my family, my wife, a very smart woman, was paying close attention. She knew and still knows my every nuance and feeling. It was because of this bond, this marriage based on love, that she saved my life that day in the change-room. There is no doubt that your loved ones are affected; let's be clear about that. If you find yourself in the pit of mental struggles or abusing numbing drugs of any kind, your family likely knows. In my case, welcoming them in, and their willingness to stay and help me, was life-changing.

I have always considered myself a dynamic and active father in my children's lives, in the past, now and into the future, but my injury and alcoholism has had an effect. We are still very close, and I sit down with them regularly to make sure there are no more secrets. Most importantly, I have apologized to them, and explained my symptoms, triggers and the disease. These explanations were simply providing them with information and were not given as an excuse. I have owned my behaviour. My message and goals now are very simple in the lives of my family. I have acknowledged the past, but we all understand that what is done is done. The only control I have or they have is what happens today, and my behaviour and reactions now. I am working every day on coping and dealing with my conditions in a transparent manner. I have relapsed, and I have tried to lie again to cover them up, but I keep getting on the horse and trying again. My family sees how hard I work at recovering from my PTSD and alcoholism every day. They recognize my triggers and mood swings as I do and I work at handling them more efficiently than in the past.

My children are adults now and very keen, aware and smart. While I know the past will always be a part of their memories, by improving every day and working with them, I continue to plant new memories as well, more positive ones. My family and I work every day in our relationships, as any family does. Kathy and I strive to set a positive example for our kids of just what our love and family has accomplished because of it. Once I asked for help, Kathy became the beaming example for our children to follow. In order for Kathy to show me such love and patience and guide our children through this journey positively, I first needed to surrender the demons and break the chains of stigma I placed on myself. I gave my family a chance to help me by letting them in and trusting them. In return, I am alive today. As my range of trust grew, I let more family members in, doctors in, and even some friends. Their love and acceptance gave me power, strength and the attitude to work hard through the battles.

I have experienced so many milestones since putting down my gun in the change-room; milestones that I would have missed. My family is proud of me every day for reaching out for help. I watched both of my children graduate high school and move on to university. My daughter has completed her studies at the University of Waterloo and will graduate with a Pharmacy Doctorate. My son has completed 3 years of a Science/Biology major program at Nipissing University, and was accepted to the School of Optometry and Vision in the fall of 2021 to achieve his Doctorate in Optometry at the University of Waterloo. I am watching and experiencing all of this. Kathy and I celebrated our 25th wedding anniversary on May 27th, 2020, and I was alive for that as well. The angels in my life are not only spiritual but also human and loving.

My recruit graduation picture taken in March 1994.

Daryl Vaillancourt, a long-time friend and a catalyst to my work with the OSPCA. He is an amazing person, and he continues to be an important part in the communities he serves, both as a citizen and on council.

Mary Davis, a childhood friend, who introduced me to the amazing Kate MacDonald and began my journey with the OSPCA.

Kal was playing with one of his chew toys, and we were able to capture this picture of what looks like a full teeth smile. He is such a ham for the camera.

Tom McVey. Tom is currently a Detective Staff Sergeant in the Crime Section of the OPP. He is also an amazing human being and cares for everyone he meets. He is a family man, but also a people person. He has the ability to manage human resources and support them. A rare find during my time with the OPP.

Emily Pearson and her kiddies; Emily was the situation that can create havoc in one's mind. In her case, she battled and survived a horrific collision as a pedestrian. She continues to include me in her life, not only on the anniversary of her crash, but any time she is through North Bay. She, her husband and family are very important to my story. Visit me on Facebook for additional pictures of the people in my journey.

AFTER HOMEWOOD

---•◦•---

July 2013, I was released from Homewood Treatment Centre after successfully completing the program. I was told of a very happy and hopeful period called being on the "pink cloud." I was on that pink cloud. I had faced addiction, I was in treatment for Post Traumatic Stress, and I was heading home to be with my family. The doctors from Homewood sent me home with a letter for the OPP giving me a few more weeks off to adjust, and then my local doctors would assume my care. I was feeling rather positive and hopeful that by asking for help, my path was now paved. My family gave me hugs, love and much admiration. I was elated to be with them again. We celebrated with an all-you-can-eat chicken wings bonanza, my go-to meal for all celebrations. I forwarded the letter to the OPP HR hole, did what was suggested, and rested. I attended AA meetings every day, found a temporary sponsor and went to regular PTSD treatment sessions with a psychologist. I got actively involved in what I needed to do to heal and move forward.

About a month later, my father and I travelled to Orillia and met with Deputy Commissioner Vince Hawkes for lunch. The conversation was great; he appeared empathetic, understanding and was going to provide me with a working environment back at my home location. This would give me the chance to succeed while integrating back into work after this long and stressful battle. He explained he would call the chief superintendent of my region, and have me re-assigned to the headquarters as a "Crime Analyst". It would be a job off the front line, but would utilize all of the skills and training I had received over the past 20 years in various roles. It was a win-win for both the OPP and for me.

I hit a very large roadblock. The North East Region Headquarters did not follow any of the directives regarding my return, nor did they offer any empathy to help a senior member return to work in a suitable role. The chief superintendent was in retirement mode, and the superintendent was in the, "I want to take over as the chief superintendent" mode. From there I endured three years of hell. I felt shame, bullying, and domination by a group of managers. The superintendent, who soon did become the chief superintendent, took off his sheep's clothing after the promotion and showed himself to be the wolf. He began to make a brand of Kool-Aid that all staff members had to drink before a promotion would be even considered. His heavy handed and cruel management style would be the standard, and the little rats followed the pied piper in plain sight. The well-meaning deputy commissioner who became our commissioner was ignored on more than one occasion, proving my earlier point about the OPP silo system and its inherent flaws. The OPP has over 8000+ members across our vast province, and this constable was being kicked around at will, and no one, not even my association, which is very large and very powerful among professional associations, did a thing to save me. The mighty OPP and my association took out their policy books and drowned me in the process.

I was cleared to go back to work medically and provided the doctor's note detailing the re-integration. However, the OPP would not let me go back to work. They needed to ask more clarifying questions; they needed more direction. It was a joke; it was the OPP way of strong-arming the employee to come back to work. They were quite aware I was running out of sick credits, and if I did not get back to work, I would stop being paid. They use this tactic all the time; not just on me. They even sent the same questions to my medical doctor and psychologist. Neither of them knew, which is another ploy that I called the OPP on. Fortunately, that practice was later stopped. The sad part of all of this is that health information questions are in place to delay and paint someone so far into a corner that they are stifled, cannot breathe, and cave in. They allege that these questions cannot be a personal diagnosis, just information they need to help me in the workplace. Over the years, the OPP knew everything about my health conditions and have asked for diagnoses on many occasions. The only things they do not know about me are my blood type and whether or not I am circumcised.

That pink cloud I was on, which for some people can last a very long time, turned grey to black within a couple of months thanks to the OPP's executive managers. When I finally returned to work in mid-October 2013, the OPP had already chipped away enough of my pride and self-esteem that instead of coming back strong and proud, I was ashamed and felt like a failure. Their decisions, as they related to me, were the same way as ripping off the scab on a wound while it is trying to heal. They continued to move my office around the building. They changed my office locations 6 times in less than three years. The executive assistant needed my space to benefit the workings of the manager, so I packed up and moved across the hall and a few doors over. Then a new sergeant position was created so she needed my office. This move made my transition even worse. To benefit the new sergeant, the chief superintendent personally had me assigned to a cubicle in the middle of the crime section of the building. The crime team was a team I used to be a part of, and I knew most of the members personally. Not only was that an environment that created triggers, but it was also in disregard to my medical requirements of being in an office with a quiet work environment. To top this situation off, they moved my office to this cubicle while I was away on vacation. I came to work, saw that my name plate was removed from the door, and I had to walk around looking for my belongings. My supervisor at the time, a staff sergeant, was not aware of the change and advocated for me with the chief, but to no avail. He said, "how do you know you cannot work there, if you don't try?" I have been trying to survive for years; he did not care or could not be bothered with my essential medical needs. The medical notes were clear, and he knew, hell, everyone knew, I would not last out in the work environment with the crime specialists.

After a significant panic episode in the cubicle, requiring additional treatment and time off, they moved me to an office used for interviewing, on the main floor where I was totally alone. No one had an office in this location. It had a door and was quiet; it was perfect. Then within a week, I realized that our training centre which was on that floor, was a pretty active place. Every uniformed member who attended the HQ for training had to line up down the hall in front of my office for an inspection by our command staff. Every uniformed member walked by, or stood by, my office door. I could not feel any worse about myself if I tried. Hundreds of officers, over time, would see Accommodated Shawn sitting in an interview room away from all other staff, my heart and mind were breaking.

During this three-year nightmare under the management of the North East Region OPP, there were a couple of positives. The analyst position was starting to take off across the province, and units were being formed. The crime side of the house at the region appointed a detective sergeant to work with me, and we were to confer with other regions and then submit a proposal for our program. This man was Tom McVey. We had worked together a little bit when he was a detective in Almaguin Highlands and I was a detective with the RACT team. Other than being told he was a good guy, I really did not know him. Turns out, everyone was right. He was a great guy, a kick-ass, hard working police officer, a family man, who cared for everyone he had contact with. When anyone talked to Tom, they could feel him listening to them. Few people I have met have what he has. His ability to be a manager in our zoo while caring and empathizing with his subordinates and superiors, is an example of some of the excellent people who are part of the OPP. He has now been promoted to Detective Staff Sergeant Tom McVey, and he still calls me for coffee every month or so to chat, even though I have not been at work or worked for him for almost four years. Tom treats me like a human with an injury. He recognizes my past work and training, and his communication skills made me believe in myself again. I worked so hard for that man just because I did not want to let him down. The neat part about Tom is that he treats everyone the same way. Whether you are uniform, civilian, crime or traffic, Tom sees the person and the employee. He is a model of how an executive manager should act. We have good people, I know a lot of them, the problem is they are not getting promoted as regularly as the Kool-aid crew ass-kissers.

Once Tom came on board and moved over to the North East Region HQ, he moved my office back upstairs to be a part of the crime team, right next door to him. I had a door, I had a window, and Tom made it clear that whoever wanted work done by me was to go through him. It was exactly what I medically needed for months and months. The analyst position was taking off, and I was enjoying it. I was helping with investigations and field support, but in a technical role instead of a field role. Sadly, my wounds were improving so, in true OPP fashion, it was time to tear the band-aid and scab off again. The powers-that-be decided to rearrange the analyst program and have the analysts at each detachment. I would be the North East Region analyst, who worked primarily for the region members and staff sergeants. They would identify a member at each detachment location. Our team was growing and Tom and I were a big reason why. You can bet how shocked I was when they told me that I belong to the North Bay Detachment and I would have to go there and do front-line analytics! My position code was my position code; I was assigned as a front-line member, not a regional member. So, once again my world was rocked. The countless health information packages were basically forgotten. I say 'rock my world' because as someone with PTSD, I could not handle or process what was happening. I was finally in a world of routine, with a manager that filtered my assignments, I was not drinking, and I was getting help. With a flick of the wrist, and without even giving my injury and medical needs a second thought, they sent me into a tailspin, just like that.

In a manner only Tom could deliver, he sat me down and broke the news. I began to cry, I was dumbfounded, and I was shocked. Tom's expression of empathy and silence was brilliant. I felt supported and understood while not babied. I told him I could not go back to the detachment, walk in the front doors, and hear the radio and my friends being dispatched to calls. I left work early that day and went straight to the beer store. Those who do not understand mental health and addictions issues would think perhaps that I chose to go to the beer store, or I chose to handle my stress and trauma flashback like this. I did not. Addictions are the go-to when untreated and even more deadly and relied upon when intertwined with mental health issues. I was right back to darkness and saw no options. After so much sobriety and work, in a flash, it was gone. I chugged six tall cans of Ice Beer in 20 minutes. Instant numb, and instant peace, yes, but guilt, shame, and anger flooded my mind once the glow faded. I was mad that I let these bastards break my sobriety, and I was so ashamed I could not tell anyone, even my family. As a result, the lying, hiding and isolation began all over again.

I continued to fight my active addiction; it is amazing how my old habits and cloaking methods came right back to me. As time went on, they hit me hard again. This time the scab had not even begun. Tom came into my office and closed the door. His face told me that he was instructed to break my heart, but it was breaking him as well. He explained that a detective whose position was assigned to Region HQ needed to be removed from active duty for non-health-related issues for a period of time, and that I was being instructed to train him on how to do my job, and that I was being sent back to the detachment. I fucking lost it. I was spun out of control. I told Tom I wanted to see the chief immediately. Tom did what a manager should do. He recognized I was gone psychologically, so instead of trying to "calm" me down, he brought me to the acting chief superintendent. Tom let speak to the source of this ridiculous decision. I am assuming he knew nothing else would have helped me in that moment, other than to let me go. I love that man for being the man he is.

I say acting chief superintendent because our chief was away and the superintendent made the decision. Tom walked me to his office, and I was in. He could see my face, and my body language was so discombobulated and erratic, he knew I was in full trigger mode. Even though he knew how much pain I was in, and even though I had worked for him before when he was a detective staff sergeant, he was able to tell me nothing. This is a man who knew and respected my father, as well as received counsel from my father during his career. He said the direction was coming from higher than him and his hands were tied. I can recall this encounter as if it happened yesterday. I was crying and hyperventilating while trying to speak. I told him that if he was getting pressure to place another member, why was he screwing me to do it? Could he not think of alternatives? The meeting was short, I was a mess and he said he would look into it some more and make a phone call. I was now a ticking time bomb, and these managers should have known better. No one cared, except Tom, a sergeant who in his professional and dedicated manner showed me empathy and fought for me, unfortunately, it was almost not enough.

I came back to work a few more days because I did not want people to think I went off work because I was being a baby. I still cared what people thought about me, and it has kept me sick a lot longer than I should have been. I went on a secretive drinking run that lasted months. These secrets affected my family again, and I went straight to the darkness. This time the darkness felt so empty. I asked for help. I started receiving support, and then the OPP executives started not just chipping away at my healing process, but blew it up. I wanted to work, and I had the skills to do work, but my value as a person hit rock bottom the minute I said the H-word in the name of mental health. The managers led the way by treating me like shit, and then over 80% of my friends and colleagues of the OPP followed their lead. I was now an alcoholic member with work-related mental health injuries who was a pariah to everything I held dear.

When you sit in the darkness, it is a mysterious place. Sadly, I have been there often, but this visit was different. Instead of drinking as I would normally do, I went for a ride in my vehicle. I had a V6 Toyota Camry and it could fly. I headed southbound on Highway #11 from North Bay and simply put the pedal to the floor. My vision blurred with tears and my head spun with anger, resentment, and disappointment. I remember the speedometer touching 180km/h and knew from my experience at crash scenes that at this speed an impact to a rock probably would not even hurt, it would be almost an instant death. This is the first time I had thought about suicide since the change-room. It was the first time I looked right, left, forward and behind and saw nothing. Thanks to the treatment centre and to AA meetings, I knew I wanted to live and these feelings were probably fleeting and needed to be challenged. I pulled the car over on the shoulder of the road and just broke down. It was at this moment that I finally understood why other members killed themselves. The pain of asking for help was not worth the accompanying bullshit, or so I thought.

As I sat on the side of the road, my thoughts turned back to the H-word, and that to use it showed more strength than anything else I could do. For reasons I still cannot tell you, I called my wife's sister, Lynn Buffett, an ER nurse, and asked if we could meet for a coffee to talk. I met a short while later with Lynn and her husband Doug, and I explained the darkness I was feeling again. After a short conversation, she urged me to go to the hospital and seek crisis intervention for my safety. I of course, fought that suggestion until my wife was off work at 7:00 PM that night. When Kathy heard of my thoughts, my call and the conversation, she joined in on insisting I go to the hospital. I finally relented, and we headed to the hospital, the whole gang of us. We arrived shortly after 8:00 PM. At the registration desk, I explained my diagnosis and current state; I was triaged and escorted to the crisis intervention interview room, with tears, anxiety, panic and shame. Kathy, Lynn and Doug stayed with me, they knew me, they were scared. I had been in this very room with people I had apprehended under the Mental Health Act as a police officer. To say I was uncomfortable, embarrassed and pissed off was an understatement. I was in the very room I brought "suffering" people to as a police officer; this time I was that person. I know the protocol; I know the system. We are waiting for a crisis worker to come in to interview me or assess me before I see the doctor. The very fact I reached out and asked for help was a huge step; agreeing and driving to the hospital was terrifying and humbling. Describing my current career, diagnosis and feelings to a triage nurse was practically unbearable, but what followed next, while waiting in that room, was nearly life-threatening.

I had already asked for help and went to a treatment centre. I was in severe distress, a flight risk and had just admitted to the thoughts of suicide. We sat in that room for over two hours, waiting for the crisis worker. I was told they were busy. I was pacing, raging, and I wanted to leave. My family talked to me, guided me and tried to keep me calm. I was in full crisis mode. I was in a crisis intervention room at the hospital, and I felt scared, ignored, and not cared about, yet again, by our system. If I came in with chest pains, a broken bone, or knife sticking out of my back, would I have to wait this long? No, I would not, because a mental health crisis is held in a different regard than a physical crisis. There was no one talking to me, no ordered medication, no monitoring, just isolation with scared family members. Just before 10:30 PM, the nurse came in to tell me I would now have to wait until the 11:00 PM shift change to see a crisis counsellor. Nope, I could not process that. I grabbed the hospital bracelet, ripped it off, threw it on the floor, and told my family I was leaving. They tried to calm me down, but they could see I was gone. I walked out of the hospital with my family in tow. No one from the hospital followed, no one even knew, and no one even cared. My life was not even on their radar; medical experts let me just flounder and walk out of their care in total rage, despair and in complete chaos. I went home with my wife, and tried to sleep. My wife could not sleep, she was afraid I was going to leave and do God knows what. Seeing Kathy so distraught and scared and me still feeling such despair, I decided to go back to the hospital.

I was back at the hospital just before 12:30 AM. I met with a crisis worker and an ER doctor. They were fantastic. The ER doctor had the knowledge, and obvious experience, to understand I was in distress. This doctor spoke to me in a professional and empathetic manner. At the end of our discussion, I was prescribed a sleeping medication and an idea that perhaps a PTSD service dog would help me. I was unable to sleep, to rest my mind. This tired and vigilant behaviour was sucking the energy out of me, leaving me susceptible to more anxiety and panic triggers.

Shortly after 2:00 AM, I was back in bed with Kathy, with medication on board. Before I could fall asleep, my mind wandered to a passing comment made by the doctor near the end of our conversation; a PTSD service dog. I fell asleep and slept for over 10 hours.

KAL – WONDER DOG

I had heard of the magic a service dog can do for people with an array of medical issues, but for me too? I started to research everything I could relating to the subject. I started to learn that certain training techniques and the various services one of these dogs can provide were in the areas I was struggling with. Crowds, hyper-vigilance, freezing, social distancing (people getting too close in a line), flashbacks, night terrors, and so much more. I was dumbfounded. I read as many articles and experience stories as I could find. I spoke with my treating psychologist and medical doctor and they both could not have agreed more. They both wrote letters of support and recommendations to obtain a trained PTSD service dog, a prescription if you will. It could be the exact link I needed to continue with my recovery, to go hand and hand with treatment sessions and sobriety.

I contacted my association and asked them if they could recommend a particular agency I could contact to see about obtaining a service dog. They provided me with three organizations that worked with military and first-responders. I researched them and reached out to a not-for-profit organization called United by Trauma. They were a volunteer, first-responder organization for PTSD. One of their outreach programs was called Ernie's Journey, where they donate Trauma Service Dogs to first-responders affected by PTSD. In short order I received a return email from one of the founders, Nicole Simard. She is a military veteran and an operating room nurse in the Greater Toronto Area. She acknowledged my email and advised they were receiving applications. They had dogs currently, and the dogs were about to be trained as PTSD service dogs.

United by Trauma raised the money, with their main earnings coming from their annual I Rock I Run fundraising event. United by Trauma (U by T) selected the recipient applicant. The process included an application, interview, doctor diagnosis confirmation, profession confirmation, a home visit and final decision. The process was run by U by T. During the interview and home visit, the dog trainer attended to discuss the actual implications an animal would have in your current lifestyle situation and whether or not a dog would be suited to help me with my particular triggers.

My direct contact during this process was Nicole Simard. She was an angel and kept me informed of the process, timelines and decisions at each level. After the process was complete, in late Fall 2015, I was selected to receive a service dog. I was over the moon excited. At that time, the dogs were being trained and were a few months old. They would remain with the trainer until they were a year old, and then the selection of the dog to the recipient would take place based on needs, the proper fit, and bonding. Through Christmas and into the New Year, Nicole kept me posted periodically on the puppies, and checked in to see how I was doing. She knew I was excited for the dog, and knew how much the dog would help me. She took immense gratification in knowing that she was helping another person suffering from PTSD. I was a stranger to her, yet she and U by T would be funding a fully trained service dog so that I could have a better quality of life. That is the definition of a hero to me.

In early February of 2016, my family travelled to the Oshawa area for my son's badminton tournament. I placed a call to Nicole and asked if perhaps we could stop by the training facility where the dogs were, for a visit. Without hesitation, she agreed and drove to the training facility to meet us there. I then met with the trainer I would have 95% of my experience dealing with, Shai Perlmutter. Shai is now the owner/operator of his own dog training facility called Evolution K9. While we were there, we were introduced to some beautiful puppies, around 6 months old. They allowed my family and me to interact with them. Their training was astounding, even at such a young age. This visit allowed my family, in particular my wife, an opportunity to see the behaviour and demeanor of the dogs. Kathy was terrified of large dogs because she had been bitten in the face as a child. Having Kathy interact with numerous German

Shepherds at once helped her manage her emotions, and even helped calm her reservations. This was an important step. It was also another example of how much support and love I had from her.

The next time I met my furry friends was in May 2016. I was invited to Shai's facility for three days of interaction and observation with the dogs. At his facility were Belgian Malinois, and Czech, Black and East German Shepherds. There were other dogs around as well. His facility was amazing. There was an indoor training area, gorgeous protected outside large pens and acres and acres of property. On our first day together, we stayed on the property, and I had the opportunity to run quite a few of the dogs through obedience and heel exercises. They were about 10 months old and their precision was mind-blowing. What was so important about this session was that Shai was able to teach me how to handle the dogs appropriately. It was quite obvious that the dogs and Shai were teaching me the ropes, not the other way around. The dogs were never treat-trained, their reward was affection and praise. At 10 months old, when I looked into any of their eyes, with the leash in hand, I could sense they had my back. These dogs were a gift.

On the second day, after some more instruction, we headed to a nearby city in the Greater Toronto Area, to see them in action in public. Stepping into highly populated areas was huge for me. I had issues at the malls in North Bay which, compared to large cities, were relatively small. The three-floor massive mall was freaking me out as we rolled up to it. Shai arranged for another police officer from a nearby municipal police service to join us on that day. He was well versed in PTSD in first-responders. The three of us arrived, along with two of Shai's dogs. I was initially given a black Shepherd, and the other police officer handled the second dog. With Shai close by, I began to walk the corridors of this busy building; I noticed almost immediately how everyone was staring at me. This made me uncomfortable at first, but I soon realized that having a big German Shepherd wearing a vest that read "Service Dog" helped keep the public away from me. Being stared at is nothing new for a uniformed police officer; you'd think we had two heads. We did a tour with the Black Shepherd, then I switched off and worked with the East German Shepherd. There was quite a difference between the two dogs, not in obedience and training, but in attitude, presence and awareness. By the end of this day, we had tackled the entire complex including the food courts, elevators and escalators. Those dogs were on point, never distracted and gave me a sense of some security. I have to admit, I was still triggered most of the day. I was soaked in sweat and was glad to walk out of that place. Still, during this short training exercise, the very fact that I even walked into that building was a huge accomplishment for me personally.

The third and final day were demonstrations of their acuteness to ignore distractions and stay on point and on command. A few of the demonstrations that I participated in were walking the dog through a set up course, with treats and cut up wieners scattered about the layout. Another exercise included instructing the dogs to go into a down-stay, this was where they laid down and were told not to get up or move. We then walked about the room, stepped over them, handled food and even walked away. These dogs did not move until given the okay by Shai. They were only 9 and 10-month-old puppies, and their attention to detail and handler awareness was incredible. For another drill, Shai had me walk the dogs through the layout and the basic commands of heel, sit, stay etc., at the same time he blasted an air compressor ratchet tool intermittently. The dogs were not startled, they just looked at me for the next command.

I would say, though, one of the most pleasant things I was able to see during this little three-day event was just how happy and free the dogs were. Every morning before we started, the dogs were brought out on their morning walk as a group; a pack. Sometimes 8 and 10 at a time. They played, ran and acted like happy ten-month old dogs. The dogs were not robots; they were well-trained dogs, skilled in helping people with medical issues. They loved it. It was like they could look straight into your soul and know how to help. To see them complete tasks and get rewarded by an ear scratch, or a verbal 'good boy / good girl', was comforting. These dogs were happy, well looked after, well trained, and quite a sight to see running amok through the bush.

As the dogs approached their first birthday, Nicole kept me and three other chosen candidates up-to-date on the remaining process. Then the call came from Shai that I would be coming to his, and his then partner's, training area in a rural setting just outside of Ottawa for dog selection. I would be in Ottawa for two weeks, beginning July 2nd, 2016. My only issue; how was I going to pay for this? All of the expenses, from transportation, hotel, meals, and dog requirements, including their food, were my responsibility. I was off work at the time, on short-term sickness, and was not being paid a full salary. My wife and I were struggling with the day-to-day expenses, due to the years of frugality and coldness brought on by the OPP. I didn't know what I was going to do. I had mentioned earlier about how mental illness treatment and physical illness treatment were not treated, or looked at, the same. Not one person, from the hundreds of members who knew me, even thought about the additional financial struggles that would be placed on me and my family. Many members at the North East Headquarters knew I was going away and that I would be returning to work with a service dog. No one offered to set up a fundraiser at the office to help financially. There was no Go Fund Me page started, no t-shirt sales, and my unit and all my co-workers never called or inquired if I needed help financially or if my family needed anything while I was gone. Nothing. These types of fundraisers happen regularly for every other member, whether uniformed or civilian, who has experienced an injury, collision, or sickness. Why wouldn't they think to offer it to someone experiencing mental health struggles? I was, and to this day I am, crushed and saddened that I was simply out of sight, out of mind. I was staying at a hotel in Kanata that had a kitchenette inside of it to help with my costs, but you can imagine what the total bill was when I was done. I was there until July 11th, 2016. 9 nights in a hotel and all the other expenses. I got myself a Mastercard and simply charged it all. A debt that took Kathy and me a few years to pay off. I digress.

I arrived at the training facility at about 1:00 pm on July 2nd and was introduced to the three other first responders who were there for the same reason I was. I also met Shai's partner at that time and was given a tour of the grounds. Most impressive indeed. An entire agility area, with at least eight or so pieces of equipment, including the eight-foot wall, jumping courses and a walking beam, just to mention a few. Most of that afternoon was welcoming us all, reviewing the agenda for the two weeks, and meeting a few of the beautiful dogs. I had some trepidation when I first arrived. Until I walked out of my car, I thought I would be there alone, with only a few dogs and the trainer, like the last couple of times I stopped in. However, those feelings did not last long, as the other participants were just like me. I was able to feel comfortable in a way where I did not feel judged, and at this time in my life, that was huge.

I was at the training facility and the hotel for a total of ten days. During that time, I was given the opportunity to work with quite a number of dogs, as the trainers observed. The goal was to pair the best dog for the specific needs of the individual. There was a female Czech German Shepherd named Luna. My family and I had met her a few times. She was sweet, had a soft demeanour and was very friendly. One of her big ears even hung down a bit, making her unique. I worked with her, as well as other types of German Shepherds and Belgian Malinois. During the training, we went off-site to public areas, large malls, as well as shopping courtyards. All areas I really hated to be in. I was with the other participants, the trainers, and the dogs, so I felt safer, but not full of happiness, to be sure.

The trainers noted something about me during these sessions. I was very anxious and always at code orange, closer to code red out in public; very hyper-vigilant. I was always at the ready, my head on a swivel, my body against the hall walls and making sharp tight turns around corners. As I worked with the dogs, it became apparent some of them were not going to fit. I needed the dog to make me feel safe, look around and be my eyes; I needed a dog with a strut. I have a lot of auditory triggers, and the dog needed to be keen to those sounds and find the source of them for me fast. If the dog jumped when I jumped, that was not helpful. Unfortunately, Luna was not my girl, the trainers told me so. They had another dog in mind, a dog I had never really met before. Kal.

Kal is an East German Shepherd working dog and is stunning to look at. He is mostly black with a blond undercoat and streaks around his head. His eyes are a piercing yellow-gold, and his ears are straight as an arrow. If I saw this animal in the dark, I would need to change my underpants. He can stare the scare into anyone. And at 11 months old, he was a month younger than most of the dogs we were working with. He is an alpha-male with an attitude and a definite strut. The trainers asked me to work with him for a while. He was amazing, but at the start really did not care for my commands or requests. When the group was walking, and we had our dogs at a heel, he would pull my fat ass to the front of the line, regardless of my heeling requests. The trainer had to show me how it was done numerous times. When I had Kal at the start, he walked where he wanted, sat and laid down on his timetable and only had interest in the trainer; but I liked him. I could see the qualities the trainers told me about. When the dogs were playing around together or out on free range hikes, he was the social one of the group. Always the one to start a play-fight, always wanting to be chased and had a happiness about him that I just adored.

During the training sessions we sometimes broke up into smaller groups, one trainer to two officers and dogs. My trainer was always Shai, and Kal loved Shai. Whatever Shai said or signalled via hand motions, Kal responded with precision. At first, with me, he answered my commands by putting his middle claw up, and smiling. Shai began to work with Kal and me alone, almost like a transfer of bond. I needed to determine if Kal would respond to me, and me independently. The more we worked, the more he began to respond. I started taking Kal back to the hotel with me at night, feeding him and brushing him. There were times I would just stare at this beast in the hotel room. I would take him out in the field near the hotel, off-leash and on-leash, and practice my commands. As I mentioned, these dogs are not treat-trained at all, ever. Their reward is love and affection. When Shai would give a command, it was obeyed. Then after a session, Shai would change his voice into a playful congratulatory tone, scratch his ears and get down to his level. That was what Kal wanted from his partner. I knew I had to work on that for him.

If anyone was watching me, they would think I was a bit bonkers. I over embellished my praise and affection, even for basic commands. When we were in the hotel room, I talked to Kal like a roommate, and he would just stare into my soul with those eyes. We were bonding, and it was magical. This beautiful animal loved me, and I could feel it. When we got back together with the group, and especially around Shai, I really needed to work on keeping him focused on me. He started to look at me during the sessions, listen and react. He still had the occasional desire to lead the pack and pull me around, but they were getting less and less frequent. We worked on his specific training around what he could do to help me with my triggers and reactions to those triggers.

I ended up staying behind an extra day and a half after the others had left. Kal was the youngest; we wanted to make sure we were both ready before we went home together. One of Kal's natural skills is the way he walks with me. He does not do a typical heel, which is generally immediately to the handler's left. Kal likes to walk a few steps in front of me. The trainer and I could have worked on getting him to that perfect heel, but I loved it. Kal had the attitude, and I felt he was saying, 'I got you, let me check out stuff before you get there.' Basically, no one could walk up to me; he is first around a corner, or an aisle, and he can split a crowd and get me through it like a hot knife though butter. He still leads the way today. He does not pull, he just leads. The other thing he does is react to noise and motion. If we are walking and we hear, or if he only hears, a noise behind me, he rotates his ear and, if needed, takes a peek. If he is fine with whatever or whoever is there, I am able to keep walking without looking myself, or planting my back against a wall. I trust Kal. There are times when Kal has not been happy with whatever or whoever is behind me. At these times he will stop, turn and stare at the person, which usually makes them take a wide berth around me – awesome! He's only been vocal with someone on 3 occasions. He did not lunge or pull, he simply gave two to three sharp deep barks. I really pay attention to those. Shai always says, 'trust the dog'. I will admit that because Kal is not vocal very often, I nearly shat my pants those three times he used his voice. I'm pretty sure the three people he barked at nearly did, too.

The final test Shai wanted me to complete with Kal was crazy. I only say crazy because I needed to make sure that Kal trusted me, obeyed my commands and came only when called. We went down to a docking area near a beach of the Ottawa River. It was a sunny and hot day, but very windy and wavy. There were a series of floating docks that resembled fingers. Basically, there was a long 50-foot dock, with additional 20-foot docks attached on either side. The docks were rocking, as they were floating docks, and there were no boats tied to them. My task was to walk out onto the dock with Kal, pick a finger, walk to the end of it, have Kal sit, and unleash him. I was then told to have him 'stay' and walk back to the shore. I am not exaggerating when I say the docks were moving. I felt unbalanced walking on them. I unleashed Kal, verbally told him to stay while showing him the hand signal for the command. I then turned around and walked away from him. I did not look back; I looked into Shai's eyes to see if he gave any information away with his reaction. I got to shore and turned around. There was my rockstar, looking back at me, bobbing away on the dock, waiting for the next command. I gave him the hand signal to come, and he came right to me in a shot. I praised the hell out of him. I then told him to go play, which means he can just go and be a dog, and of course the first thing he did was go into the Ottawa River. I did not know German Shepherds loved water so much. Kal loves the water.

On July 11th, 2016, I loaded Kal into the back seat of my Toyota Camry Sport, and travelled home. I have so many Kal stories that I will touch on going forward. Needless to say, Kal has been a life-changer, and at times, a life-saver. This alpha-male, East German Shepherd is a gift I received from Nicole Simard and the volunteer crew at United by Trauma. Their gift, while I did not know it on that day, would propel me into giving back as well.

Kal and I are Home

While I was driving home, I kept looking in the rear-view mirror at the beast in the back seat, and I was awestruck and in disbelief. I was going to be arriving home before Kathy got off work, so I went to my parent's house first to see my sister Sherri who was visiting from Nova Scotia. It was pulling into their driveway that my father witnessed Kal in work mode. I opened the door to the backseat to release the hound. My father loves dogs and is not afraid of them. My dad was happy to see me, especially because I had this gift of a service dog. My dad walked right toward me, and Kal intercepted. He stepped right between my dad and I. I called Kal's name, and my dad slowed his approach, and the introduction was made peacefully. I knew then that we were bonded for sure.

After a short visit, I head home right away, anxious to see Kathy and excited for her to meet Kal. When I arrived, I introduced him to our 10-pound wiener dog, named Zoey. Zoey has the same colour pattern as Kal, and at the age of 10, she was not amused at his presence. Kal approached her to smell her, and she blew a gasket, snarling, growling and lunging at him. Kal backed up, looked at me like, "Hey, what the hell is her problem?" Kal left her alone; they took their time, and now they are best of friends. They now sleep side by side; Kathy and I walk them together (you should see the looks we get), and as long as Kal understands he comes second in the house, Zoey accepts him. However, if Kal bugs her or approaches Kathy or one of the kids with Zoey on their lap, she growls and tells him off. Kal teases a bit, then walks away. I swear he does it on purpose sometimes.

I was in the kitchen when Kathy walked into the house. Our entrance has a small landing, then three steps leading up into the main living area. Kal was standing at the top of the three steps, staring at Kathy. Kathy froze in fear. Kathy was not expecting this alpha male beast; she expected a smaller female Shepherd, like Luna. I started towards the entrance when I heard Kathy in a quiet but urgent voice say, "Shawn come get your dog". Kathy and Kal are now very close, and that is because Kathy put her legitimate fears aside for me, knowing this large dog was there to help me. Kal is not trained to be a guard dog. His duties are all done in a non-threatening manner. He uses his size and stare to perform most of the tasks to support me in public. I often say that anyone could punch me in the face, and Kal would not react; having said that, if anyone tried to harm Kathy he would kick their ass. That is how close they are now.

Kal developed a bond with my children as well. My daughter, who only lived with Kal for a short while, developed a kinship with him. He was very affectionate and quiet with her. She loved taking his picture and felt so much peace with him. When Shawna experienced some very serious and, at times, critical health issues that landed her in the hospital, Kal would come to the hospital with me and jump on her hospital bed to snuggle her. Kal and Shawna have an awesome bond; very similar to the nature of the bond I share with him. He recognizes her health issues and responds in a touching way. When my daughter moved to Kitchener-Waterloo to attend pharmacy school, she and Kal no longer had that day-to-day contact, but he never forgot that bond. There are times we do not see our little girl for months, but when Kal catches a glimpse of her, he runs to her with such happiness. He will jump on her shoulders and kiss her face over and over again. Here's a funny story to explain what I mean. I drove to Kitchener with Kal to pick up Shawna to bring her home for one of her breaks. I was parked in the area of the pharmacy school which is right in the heart of Kitchener. I had Kal off-leash in a field nearby after the long drive, waiting for Shawna to be finished. Then I saw her exit the back door of the school, so did Kal. Kal was about two football fields away from her at the time. He lifted his nose in the air, identified her, and then ran full-out towards her. He crossed the field, ran through the parking lot, and down the walking path towards Shawna. People were watching in both awe and fear, as he is a very quick and wolf-like looking beauty. It was almost as if the public were watching the scene, thinking, "Oh my God, that poor girl is dead!" When he arrived to her, he jumped up, putting his paws on her chest and shoulders, licking and whining in excitement. Shawna was laughing, and Kal was beyond excited. His gift to me keeps giving to my family, as well.

Kal's relationship with my son Brady is awesome. Brady is an animal lover and would have a house full of dogs if we let him. Brady is a tall lad, about 6'3", and he loves to play fight with Kal. When Brady comes home, Kal will find his toy, bring it to Brady at the door and bash his legs as if to say, "Hello!" If Brady is in bed and his door is not closed, Kal will run across the rec room and jump on his bed with excitement. He jumps on him and nibbles at his skin, and then the fight is on. Brady will lay on the floor and wrestle with Kal, and I mean, they go at it. They both love it. Their battles are legendary. If Kal is downstairs, where Brady's bedroom is and Brady comes down the stairs, Kal will set up behind the wall near the stairs, and as soon as Brady touches the floor, he will pounce, like a lion attacking a gazelle. He will wrap his big front paws around Brady's lower legs and ankles and lean hard, causing Brady to fall to the ground. The match continues from there.

I have witnessed numerous moments of Kal with my family that touched my heart. Imagine bringing a large, one-year-old German Shepherd into your house, a house where our pet is a 10-pound miniature wiener dog, hoping that the family is okay with it. I am a very lucky man that my family has embraced Kal, and not only as my service dog but also as a member of our family.

The OPP and Kal – Sadness and Disappointment Yet Again

I did not think the OPP could cause an issue over a fully trained service dog. The OPP managers at North East Region Headquarters were pathetic, shallow, and downright mean. I also want to single out our HR administrator for the region, in this category. I have detailed a few incidents where they were less than accommodating, but with respect to the service dog, their behaviour burned a hole in my memory that I cannot process still to this day. I did all the work, worked with doctors, applied for the service dog supported by the OPPA and still, they would not support me. The OPP made me feel they did not care if I was getting paid, and that they did not care to even help me with the process. This is what I was met with.

When I received the great news that I qualified for a trained service dog, I notified the management in my office. The date of delivery was still six months away. The dog trainer and Nicole Simard from U by T wanted to come to visit my office to see the layout and dynamics surrounding the work environment. This visit would help the trainer establish the training requirements for the dog. However, I, once again, received pushback from the OPP. I notified the staff of their visit, and they immediately threw up walls. They advised that the guests could come into the building, but they did not want the dogs to accompany them, as they felt they needed to survey the staff to determine if there were dog allergies in the building. Pardon? A service dog is permitted in any building; that is the law. The right to a service dog is mentioned in the Accommodations Act, an Act they made all OPP employees review through e-learning so that we knew how to treat all people regardless of any circumstance or accommodation requirements. Kal and I could walk into a grocery store, a big box store, a church or a restaurant, but not the OPP North East Region Headquarters, oh no! They first had to make sure the other 75 or so other staff in the building had a say. The dog trainers had brought down two dogs, one a fully trained service dog, the other still in training. However, the dogs had to stay outside. Here I thought this was an opportunity for others in the building to meet the dogs, to observe the dogs' quiet and reserved natures. The bottom line here is this: I can appreciate if you have an allergy to dogs, that a dog being present could be an issue, but this was a visit. It is no different than if a person with an allergy meets a service dog in a store or even a plane; the dog is a medical requirement and allowed by law to be there to fulfill their duties for the injured worker.

There was not one member of our command team that came to meet the trainer or founder of the program. They assigned a detective staff sergeant and the HR representative. They ushered us into the boardroom for a little Q & A. Fortunately, the detective staff sergeant in the room was someone I had a lot of respect for. The HR representative was unsympathetic and had judgemental questions about everything. I won't get into all of it, but needless to say, it felt like the last thing she cared about was me, or the dog. She asked questions like, "If there was a meeting in a boardroom with other people, would I need to bring the dog or could I leave it secured in my office?" Nicole Simard fielded that one, saying that is what the dog is for and it's not possible to predict when the dog would be needed. If medical aid is required at that particular moment, then yes, the dog should be there. There were also the questions about picking up the dog's bowel movements, like it was a deal-breaker. Of course, when I took the dog out, I would pick up after him, like all dog owners do, or at least should. Out of all her questions and concerns, not one of them was about how the dog would help me. At no time did I feel supported with my accommodation requirement. Once the Q & A was done, our HR representative left; the detective staff sergeant tried to salvage the visit by taking the trainer and Nicole on a tour of the building and the grounds.

He introduced them to some of the staff, and wouldn't you know, the staff asked where the dogs were, as they had heard of this visit.

When I walked Nicole and the dog trainer to their vehicle, they let the dogs run about before their three-hour trip back home. Even they were caught a bit off guard by the tone of the visit. Usually, there was excitement, and even pride, when they toured other police services. They shared that the OPP was the most difficult agency to deal with.

This next part of integration back to work for Kal and I was a disaster, leading to an alcohol relapse and never returning to work again. I was home with Kal on July 11th, 2016, because my health care experts suggested that I remain at home with Kal for two weeks before bringing him to work. So, in late July, I called to tell them I had been medically cleared to return and provided a note. They told me no, I could not come back yet. Why? They were having an inspection company from Toronto come to the North East Region Headquarters in North Bay, 3 ½ to 4 hours away, to inspect the ductwork system in the building.

During their survey with the staff about the dog, an employee indicated that they had a severe allergy to dogs. This employee has an office on the first floor of the building, I am situated on the 2nd floor of the building. This Toronto inspection company would determine where and how the air flowed through the system. The inspection still had not been completed, so I could not come back to work. I cannot make this stuff up. The money that was spent and wasted here could have been spent on positive accommodations and helping all members with PTSD requirements.

I was cleared medically, with a trained service dog, and ready to work, but I could not work; the OPP would not allow it. Also, while I was waiting for this inspection and subsequent findings, I stayed home on my sick credits, which were currently at only 75% of my wage. They can't do that, right? They did.

After the inspection was complete, I was informed that the ventilation system had two systems, depending on where you were in the building. They determined that my office on the second floor was on the same system as this employee's office on the first floor. So, I had to move my office down the hall. I mean, just down the hall; I could see my old office. I was beside my supervisor, who was doing an excellent job managing my workload, but now I had to move down the hall. To make matters worse, this office was right at our section's enter and exit door. So that meant a person with PTSD, who has an attentive service dog, was put in the office right where it was the busiest, loudest and most distracting office on the floor. Brilliant. I was moved just down the hall because of airflow circuits. I call bullshit that this would prevent any dog dander from escaping into the abyss of air circulation. The other rules I was given pertained to washrooms and the change-room. I always used to shower at work after a morning walk, but I was now told that I could no longer use the change-room because it was too close to the office of this employee. Furthermore, he had a locker in that change-room where he got ready for work. So did I. What they were saying was, because of my injury, I was not allowed to use the change-room facilities, or even walk in there with the dog. Also, the washroom on the first floor was out of bounds as well; I was to use the washroom on the second floor only. So now I know where to pee and that I cannot change at work anymore, even though everyone else, who did not have the PTSD injury, would have a choice. Just not me.

While there are so many things wrong with what I have mentioned so far, this next bit of information blows the mind. I have known this employee with the dog allergy for quite a few years. Before North Bay, we lived in the same town for a number of years. I used to drop by his house as he was into woodworking, and I was just learning. Whenever I went to his house, I would be greeted by his dog! For the entire time I knew him in this town, he had a dog, a Labrador, I believed, either way, it was a large breed. So now I was confused, but kept my mouth shut. I did not need any more bumps trying to return to work.

Finally, September 1, 2016, over a month after I was medically cleared to return to work, I reported for duty to my new office with Kal. No one from the command staff welcomed the dog and me back to work on the first day. Returning to work with Kal was a big deal. I was the first OPP uniformed member to bring a service dog to work. I was fighting and battling my debilitating injury and kept coming back. My co-workers were excited to see Kal, and he was very well received. Now, I cannot recall if it was the first day at work or the next day at work, but that first week back, I bumped into the employee with the allergy. I left my office to go to the printer, where I met up with the employee, on my floor, in my section, just down the hall from my office where Kal and I sat. I gave him a heads up that the dog was now at work with me. He said this, "Oh that is no problem; as long as I do not touch him or get his saliva on me, I am fine." Pardon? I was told the locations in the buildings I was not allowed to go was so as to not adversely affect this employee, meanwhile he had no restrictions and can wander willy nilly around the building. I could not shower or use my locker to hang up my coat and put my boots away, but he could stroll around wherever he needed to. This unbalanced support was another example of the poor leadership. Once again, the injured, mentally ill staff member was isolated. The stigma and shame around mental illness continued, but other employees with medical conditions are fully accommodated.

The OPP essentially restricted my accommodations, so another employee was accommodated? So, from what I could gather, his allergy might have been severe, but he had to have physical contact with the dog to cause a reaction. Air flow, or the dander the dog may release into the air, was never an issue. There was no need for an office change or even an inspection for that matter. Did management not ask this employee any questions? Did they have any idea how the delay returning to work, the restricted locker use and specific pee location affected my psyche? I liked this employee with the allergy, and still do. The onus was never on him, but on our leaders. They dropped the ball, and, in my opinion, they dropped the ball intentionally, as well.

I never stood a chance. September 7th, 2016, was the last day I worked at the OPP. The location of my workspace was distressing, triggering, and a major distraction to the dog and to me. Command staff treated me like a problem, and I never felt welcomed by them. They cost me so much money due to their delays and restrictions. All because I have a brain injury, PTSD, caused by my career as a police officer with the Ontario Provincial Police. Their answer over many years equalled little support and many barricades. After my third day returning to the office, I started to drink again; I drank for three consecutive days. Thankfully, because of all the hard work I had put into my recovery, I understood where I would end up. I let my family and doctors know about my relapse. My doctors deemed me permanently disabled from an injury. It was not what I wanted. Being regarded disabled and not being allowed to work was not my plan. I had dreams, I had goals, and the useless actions from the OPP halted them all. Their inaction, lack of vision and lack of compassion for its employees cut me off at the knees.

As I write this section, I have been off work now for four years, and it has only been the last year that I have finally come to peace with the situation. Over the last four years, my depression and anxiety escalated exponentially because I felt like a failure, and almost everyone at work abandoned me. Generally, the herd follows the leader, and these leaders led with shame and intimidation. As a result, others looked at me as a wimp who couldn't hack it. So untrue and so unfair. I loved my job, and I helped a lot of people. Sadly my employer wasn't there for me when I needed help.

My New Life with Kal – Service Dog

Now what? It came down to a new normal, a new normal that I was not prepared for, did not want and was ashamed of. I was told as a result of my workplace injury; I had been deemed disabled. I could no longer work as a police officer or anywhere else, for that matter. I had to try and wrap my head around that. For someone who may not quite understand the scope of my new shame and triggers, I will try and explain it to you.

On September 8th, 2016, I realized and rationalized my current situation; I was a 45-year-old married man with a daughter in university, a son about to be in first year university, and an unstable income. I was trying to coordinate getting paid by WSIB, my insurance company and disability through the CPP (Canada Pension Plan). I had little to no guidance dealing with these agencies, and my mental health was sliding into the darkness again. Having an injured worker battling through a mental health injury, such as PTSD, and trying to navigate through the bureaucratic nightmare that is our system, is asking for that member to fail and possibly give up. That was happening to me. I could not handle the unaccommodating process, continued roadblocks and unempathetic agents at the WSIB. My claim was submitted in June 2011 and was not resolved until 2019. That was eight years of being told to prove my disability. A process that continuously caused further harm to my disability. Once it was finally approved, thanks only to the first-responder legislation, my claim was retroactive to 2017. However, this also meant more challenges, such as receiving money and then being told I had to return some of it due to inaccurate equations. I had to figure out on my own what was taxable, what was not, what my tax rate was supposed to be for the CPPD (Canada Pension Plan Disability) benefit, or risk getting hit hard at tax time. Are you kidding me? I could not even decide if I was going to get out of bed or whether I should drink or not. Again, this process was not at all accommodating. This was when my angel came to the rescue again. Kathy was watching me losing my mind and had a solution.

She offered to be my representative, as the OPPA claimed they could not provide that sort of service. The OPPA merely assigned paralegals to help me. While I have great respect for the work of a paralegal, they were not equipped to handle this type of potentially fatal injury or the red tape I needed to fight. I will always refer to the paralegals' role as "hoop holders". The WSIB and my insurance company insisted on us following archaic policies that were not set up to support and assist the mentally injured, especially PTSD suffered by a first-responder. In an attempt to change the procedure, I pleaded and begged the OPPA to assign one of our lawyers to my case, and to the cases of my peers who were also dealing with this complex issue. A lawyer could help us to fight the policies, timelines, requirements, paperwork, and help us choose life, instead of committing suicide. I met with the OPPA Executive, along with my father and the local OPPA President and made a formal request to have this done. It was denied. They actually said they found that a paralegal, in these incidences, is most capable and could be less confrontational at times. Bullshit! The problem for me was the process. Moving on, what Kathy did was become my voice. I gave her full authority with the OPP, OPPA, WSIB, Great West Life (now Canada Life) and the CPPD to navigate these muddied waters. Kathy worked with my payroll department to understand when I was off payroll, which credits were kept and which were not. She questioned the WSIB, the paralegal, the OPPA, and everyone else, to explain and re-explain the process. Kathy even found an error with the OPP's summation of my vacation credits; they miscalculated and actually owed me 40 hours of pay. She let me deal with my health, and she made sure I received my benefits correctly. This should have been a job for my association. This amazing woman, who is trying to figure out how to live with a police officer suffering extreme mood swings, erratic behaviour and addiction, is now forced to be my full-time advocate. Everyone knows living with someone battling PTSD and addiction is a very difficult position. It takes the kind of love and commitment that luckily, I have in my wife. She was doing multiple roles, in addition to being my advocate: being a mother, working out of the house, and constantly worried for my safety and sobriety. Kathy Fougère is a hero not only to me but to everyone close to me.

Aside from the logistics of life I just mentioned, the way I perceived myself and my new normal was very dark. When I looked in the mirror, I saw a broken man, a man who was a disgrace to himself and his family. I was a police officer, and the entire community knew my profession; that was gone, and people were starting to ask me what I was doing now. The answer of nothing was not an appealing one. I was on brain-candy meds (anti-depressants, and pills for sleeping and for anxiety), was battling alcoholism, which I was failing at, and now a whole lot of new triggers for my PTSD. I was no longer a police officer with PTSD; I was now a former police officer, who couldn't work because of PTSD, needed drugs and booze to live each day, and had a full-grown German Shepherd with him 24/7 to cope. I hated myself. I am telling you with God's honest truth, had I known in May 2013 when I was in that change-room with my gun in my mouth, the "processes" I would have to go through and how I was feeling at his point – bang! I was even pissed off about making that promise to Kathy. I had now disclosed the change-room incident to my family; my wife made me promise that I would never try to take my life again. I made that promise. I now knew what it would do to my family. I was left broken, addicted, continually triggered, sad, angry and ashamed. I had a new service dog that I was still getting to know, and vice versa, and I had no way of making these feelings go away. I had made a promise to the love of my life, my wife.

The next few years were full of battles won and lost. I was sober and then I was not. I was truthful and then I lied about my drinking. I was seeing a psychologist as well as my medical doctor quite regularly. Kathy was worried about my safety and sobriety when she went to work. My kids were watching their dad, who was once so active, happy and goofy, become a shell of emptiness and anger. The injury and entire process of trying to get help had ruined my life. I was hosting an all-day pity party for myself that I did not recognize due to my symptoms and triggers. The only new thing in my life was this beautiful German Shepherd named Kal. I had received him as the most precious gift; I turned to him and worked with him to form an unbreakable bond. Kal started giving me back a bit of my quality of life. I worked with Kal a lot and took him everywhere with me, and I still do. I did maintenance training and still call Shai to this day to discuss issues or ask any questions I may have. Shai's contractual requirements have long been over, but he tells everyone that he is there for anyone with one of his trained dogs, and he is.

I do not have to do that much maintenance training anymore, as after four years together, we are quite in tune with one another. When I say I take Kal everywhere, I mean it. Kal has been on a large commercial flight, subway systems, a large ferry, ATV, boat, bus, church, AA meetings, restaurants, swimming pools, the Quebec City Zoo, travelled the Maritimes, a Blue Jays game, an OHL hockey game, hospitals, school ceremonies (on stage too), all of my speaking engagements, on the stage in front of 350+ people, malls, camping trailer, cars, vans, and on and on. My point, there is no place I cannot bring him. He is always on point, well mannered, engaged and very flexible. I was once on a trip to Nova Scotia from North Bay; we first flew from North Bay, on a small puddle jumper plane, to Toronto. Kal had his own seat and enjoyed the ride, laying down and amazing the passengers. When we boarded the larger 737 plane from Toronto to Halifax, the flight was full. I was with my dad, and there was a lady between us. Without direction, Kal laid down and went under the seats in front of us, he was out of the way, but I could see his face, and his eyes. That was all I needed.

Kal and I are so close because of the time we spend together. Kal knows my every nuance, and our movements when we're out and about are without issue. North Bay is a smaller city, so Kal and I are well known. What I really mean is, Kal is well known, and loved. On occasion we come across people who take issue with Kal, but 99% of the time, I find the public accepts us everywhere. The key has been Kal's training from the very beginning; a properly trained animal, specifically chosen and trained for medical service work, and not a converted pet. One of the constant challenges has been trying to adapt and accept my new reality, and Kal has been a big part of that acceptance. It took until 2018 – 2019 to even remotely accept I would no longer work as a police officer; a job I loved. I had to rationalize that my injury is an injury like any other. Once I did that, I went to work on my new passion.

I began to advocate for everyone suffering from mental illness and/or addiction. I wanted the people who were impacted like me to know that what they are suffering through is not less than any other illness. One of my first corny-type expressions to articulate this message was explaining that all injuries and illnesses were the same, in a way that mental illness may be an apple, and another type of physical injury or illness may be an orange, but while they are different fruits, they are both still fruit, thus the same. I started to talk to anyone who would ask or listen, and explain that to heal; we should view mental illness recovery as strength, and never shame. I beat shame. I am no longer ashamed of myself. That simple statement took a lot of time, treatment, work, and a dog named Kal. My opportunity for a wider audience and the beginning of giving back appeared when I ran into a childhood friend and neighbour named Mary Davis. Our professions had crossed paths a couple of years earlier at a meeting, and when Mary met me again, with Kal, at a local coffee shop, my life and life path offered a turn, and I will be forever grateful I accepted the new direction.

The Ontario Society for the Prevention of Cruelty to Animals (OSPCA)

————◆•◆————

M ary Davis and I started discussing how Kal, a service dog, was such an integral part of my mental health injury. We also chatted about my alcoholism and how I was no longer ashamed of who I was or what had happened to me during our discussion. I soon realized that Mary and I had similar passions and goals. You see, Mary is the Executive Director of the Nipissing Mental Health Housing and Support Services; mental health was her passion and life's work. Mary was also the Chair of the Board for the North Bay Humane Society. As I write this, she is also on the Board of the Ontario SPCA and Humane Society. She has a passion for animals, too. Given her background, she was really interested in the jobs Kal performs, and just how positively he has transformed my quality of life. Once Mary understood I was quite willing to share my story, she ran an idea past me. She explained that the CEO for the Ontario SPCA was a dynamic, forward-thinking and brilliant woman named Kate MacDonald. She asked if I would be willing to meet with her to discuss possibly sharing my story with the Ontario SPCA? I was more than willing to participate.

In short order, Mary called me to meet with her and Kate MacDonald at a local coffee shop to chat. When I met with Kate, it was immediately clear that I was speaking with a positive leader. She was passionate not only about the Ontario SPCA but her team of employees and bettering the lives of the animals they advocated and cared for, and all people. Kate explained that she would like me to share my story within the Ontario SPCA and its network, as she believed Kal and I had something to offer to others. She was so kind and was truly interested, fascinated and quite amazed by my story. I felt like I was being understood. It was an incredible and genuine conversation. I was speaking with two very forward thinking and out-of-the-box leaders in their field, and they felt I could and should be a part of helping others.

Within a few months, I received a call from Kate MacDonald. She asked if I would speak at a staff training session in Welland, ON. She asked me to tell my story, and the story as it continued with Kal. The meetings were a couple of months away, in October 2017. I immediately went to work and prepared a dynamic PowerPoint presentation, with photos, facts and most importantly, a full overview of what happened to me from start to finish. I had one condition, although she was more than willing to pay for my time, I insisted that I not receive any money for the presentation. The way I looked at it was that, although I was not being paid my full salary at that time, I was being paid through benefits because of my injury. In conversation with my psychologist, he recommended and endorsed my presentations as they had a treatment-style benefit. When I shared my story, I became empowered and proud of my journey. I wanted this to be from a place of love and caring for others in similar situations, and so being there on my time made it so much more personal to me.

I attended the staff training session at the Niagara SPCA and Humane Society in Welland, Ontario with a thumb drive and a computer in hand. Kate was there and I was pleased to be introduced to John Greer, Executive Director, Niagara SPCA and Humane Society. John's background was in Correctional Services so, we shared common ground. The staff, along with various guests from across the province, were there for a few days of training, and I was to be a part of their mental health training. I was honoured. The funny thing was, I was not nervous at all. I was laser-focused and looking forward to just being Shawn and Kal. Before the presentation started, I saw a familiar face, Daryl Vaillancourt, the former director of the North Bay Humane Society and at that time, the Chief, Humane Programs & Community Outreach for the Ontario SPCA. Daryl and I have known each other since our daughters started

Junior Kindergarten together, 20 years earlier. He was someone who was always involved in his community. He served many years on North Bay City Council. It comforted me to see him there with Kate, knowing that I was doing the right thing. With Kal in hand, we stepped out in front of the group, approximately 15 to 20 people. I powered up the PowerPoint and began. I spoke from my heart and mostly off the cuff, using the slides as a guide. I showed pictures of my family, my career, and my struggles.

I told them everything, even the change-room gun incident. I told them of my addictions and my battles with sobriety. I told them how low I was, and then how things started to turn around for me once I received the gift of Kal. I made them laugh, and I made them sad; I was me, and I felt stronger than I had in years. At the end of my presentation, I accepted questions, and they asked a lot of questions. To many, baring your soul and the skeletons in your closet may have been the hardest part, but for me, it made me come alive. It lasted about an hour and a half, and I received many thanks and compliments. When I returned home, Kate contacted me to tell me that everyone at the presentation was still talking about it and that they enjoyed and learned so much from me. Daryl Vaillancourt contacted me, congratulating me on a terrific job and said that he was proud to be my friend. I was blown away. My story of strength, hope, and a lot of work, informed others, and made people happy. That, my friends, is the definition of smashing shame and stigma right in the face!

This presentation started a bit of a trend. When I returned home, a Professor at Nipissing University instructing third-year students in the Criminology program, asked if I would come and speak to his class about PTSD. This man was Adjunct Professor Carson Fougère; yup, my dad. When I said I had the support of my parents, I really did. I immediately agreed. Two weeks after presenting to the Niagara SPCA, I was in a theatre-style classroom at Nipissing University in front of well over 50 people, including the students, other Professors and one of the Deans of the Criminology program. My dad gave me a very heartfelt introduction, one that hit me right in the feels. Paraphrasing, he said, "as you know, I have been a police officer for a long time, and I know a lot of police officers. I often bring in topic experts available to me through my network, but I know this speaker the best of all. This is my son, Shawn, and he is a police officer and has been diagnosed with PTSD." He is proud of me and supports me speaking out and helping others through the elimination of stigma, and normalizing mental health and addiction ailments as equals to all diseases and injuries. My wife Kathy has been my rock, to be sure, but my parents are also right there.

As I spoke, you could hear a pin drop. Again, I could make them laugh when things were getting deep, but did not shy away from my story, which was a little harder because of my dad in the room. Not because I was ashamed, but because this was the first time he heard me speak so freely, and the seriousness of my story was never more clear. When it was over, and we were alone, he gave me a bone-crushing hug. I was getting stronger by the minute. The students were very attentive, and many came to speak to me afterwards, and to meet Kal.

As part of my presentation, I always included my contact information, such as cell phone and personal email address. A couple of days after this presentation, one of the students asked to meet me for a coffee. She wanted to discuss that she was seeing in her dad, a military veteran, the same signs of PTSD I described. I met her at a coffee shop, and we just chatted. I am not a doctor or a trained counsellor, and I make that point clear when I speak. I can offer my experience, what worked for me, what did not work, and what I wish could have happened. My conversation with her was simply for her to inquire how she could start a conversation with her dad without an escalation of emotion or causing him to feel backed into a corner. This was an adult student, not a child. While I would never instruct anyone on what to do or say, I will offer what I would have wanted or not wanted. A month or so down the road, she asked my dad to tell me that she had met with, and had a conversation with, her dad and that it had gone very well.

One month later, in November, I received a call from Mary Davis, who had heard about the success of my presentation at the Niagara SPCA, and asked if I could speak with her staff. Of course, I agreed and attended their office boardroom. This time, it was a roundtable-style discussion, no PowerPoint, no notes, just an open conversation. Her staff asked such poignant questions and were really interested in picking my brain to help the clients they served. What a feeling, I was starting to help others again, as I did as a police officer.

In early 2018, I received a call from Daryl Vaillancourt and Kate MacDonald. They informed me that the Ontario SPCA was hosting their annual conference, and wanted to know if I would be willing to be a speaker at one of their breakout sessions. They shared that the conference featured a lineup of dynamic speakers from a range of areas of expertise and that the attendees included delegates from across Canada and the USA. I agreed. A couple of short weeks later, Daryl called again and asked if instead of speaking during one of their breakout sessions, would I be willing to be one of their keynote speakers. I would kick-off their second day of the conference, speaking, with Kal, for an hour and a half. I felt honoured to be invited to speak. One of their other keynote speakers was Cassie Campbell-Pascall, two-time Olympic gold medalist and broadcast commentator. How cool; I watched her on Hockey Night in Canada, now I was going to be on the same stage as her.

This conference turned out to be a turning point in my life. Not only for me as a symbol of empowerment, but it sculpted my new path in a way I would never have expected. The conference was being held at The Fallsview Resort in Niagara Falls. Kathy was also invited to join me; considering the magnitude of this speaking engagement, I really appreciated having Kathy by my side. We arrived at Fallsview on the Saturday night; we checked into a beautiful room overlooking Niagara Falls, both the American and Canadian falls. The room was arranged and paid for. We were greeted by Taryn Byrne, the organizing machine, and my contact for the event. She was amazing and treated Kathy, Kal and me in the most caring and professional way.

The next morning, we found our way down to the conference centre to register. That was when I realized that this gig was like no other. The conference hall was humongous, decorated to the hilt, and was the most professionally laid out conference I had ever attended. This massive room was adorned with roundtables with eight chairs around each one and a stage large enough for a music band to perform on. On each side of the stage were huge screens, cameras set up, and a stage crew, led by Mike Feld of Most Excellent Productions, that resembled some of the most professional groups I knew. I asked one of the people at the registration desk how many people were there suppose to be. She said probably around 350 to 375. Pardon? Kathy and I went into the room, with Kal, and both stood looking around in disbelief. Kathy asked me if I would be okay, and I said yes. I also knew that Kathy was nervous for me, and I was nervous for her reaction as well, as she had never heard me speak before. I hoped my candidness would be okay for her. The next day, all of it, Monday, June 4th, 2018, was life-altering for so many people, including Kathy and me.

OSPCA Conference Launch Pad

A s I entered the conference hall with Kathy and Kal, it was already about half full. We sat at a table with some of the members of the North Bay Humane Society and settled in. I remember leaning over to Kathy and saying something along the lines of, "Holy shit, I am not in Kansas anymore." The room quickly filled, and the murmur of chatter and laughter was everywhere. I was not nervous at all. However, I was nervous about doing a good job, not falling off the stage, that sort of thing; but standing up in front of over 300 people and talking about my mental health and addiction story didn't bother me one bit. It was a strange feeling. I met with Mike Feld and Most Excellent Productions, the awesome audio-video team, gave them my PowerPoint and got wired with a microphone. There was a podium and stationary microphone on the stage, but I had earlier asked to have the podium moved out of the way, and inquired about a wireless mic so I could walk around. I have always been an animated person when speaking, even if it's to a friend, so for me to feel comfortable, I needed the whole stage to walk around. As my introduction was being read, I remember looking at Kal and giving him a hug/tap and told him it was showtime. They called Kal and I up to the stage, and the hall erupted with clapping. Kal was not amused.

As I had mentioned before, a lot of my social triggers are auditory. A loud sudden noise, crying, especially children, sirens, radio transmissions, etc. Kal investigates all those noises for me, finds where they are coming from, and looks at me. It is so calming. Once I know the sound, where it is coming from and that I am safe, I can easily diffuse myself. This works out 99% of the time. There is however one sound that Kal does not like; it is when a group of people clap. I guess the sound is loud, but with so many points of origin, he darts around and is not amused until it stops. As I got up on the raised stage, Kal was at full attention and staring out at everyone, moving from side to side. Once the clapping ended, Kal sat down and I begin. Before I start presenting, I always tell my audience two things. The first is about Kal and his reaction to sudden noises. I explain that if it occurs not to be concerned and if he finds a way off the stage, he is doing his job, and will not engage with anyone. The second thing is that I am a very proud member of the Ontario Provincial Police, a police officer, and my presentation is my journey with mental health and addiction. This journey has come with several poor decisions and behaviours by members of the OPP brass, but does not mean I am a bitter police officer.

I need to first describe my wardrobe. I am very stalky, with broad shoulders and large neck, size 19 ½". As you can imagine, your basic box-store does not regularly carry this size of neck, so I need to search for my shirts. The other predicament I have is when I find the right neck size, they assume and construct the shirt as if I am the size of a small elephant; the shirt goes to my knees, and the arms would fit the length of arms for an orangutan. I found a few shirts at a big and tall shop that were perfect. Large neck, but normal size shirt for my arms. I was proud of the shirt I chose for this event. It was a new one, baby blue with white stripes. I wore it with khaki pants and brown dress shoes. Why am I telling you all this? I am a person that sweats a lot. I sweat putting on my socks, shaving and going for a simple walk. I did not anticipate this issue when I made my shirt selection. I had mentioned earlier, there were two wall-size TV screens on each side of the stage. I thought that my PowerPoint slides would be appearing on those screens. Nope, just a big old blow up of baby blue shirt-boy. When I put up my first slide, which I could see on a monitor at the edge of the stage, I glanced to the large TV screen to make sure it was up there. What I saw was my side profile, showing the back of my shirt, totally soaked. I instinctively blurted out, "oh, look at my back', and laughed, and so did the crowd. Perfect way to start, really it was.

As I began to tell my story, I became more confident. With each slide and photo, I could see that everyone was listening, almost locked on my every word. This is probably the first time in years where I had a sense of pride in myself again. Up until this point, I was still very much angry at myself and invited the shame of mental illness into my heart. I was getting stronger leading up to this day, welcoming my current path of speaking up and speaking out at shame and stigma towards mental health and addiction, but now I was totally empowered. The feeling was indescribable. During my talk, the crowd did laugh and at one point, clap. Kal jumped off the stage and away he went running amongst the tables. The crowd was ok with it because I warned them. Once the crowd stopped clapping, Kal ventured throughout the room and found where my wife was sitting and stayed with her for the remainder of the presentation. I could see him and he could look at me. When I made eye-contact with Kal from the stage, I noticed that Kathy had been crying, with Kleenex in hand from my presentation. So Kal went to her to be there for her support, but continued to watch me. Absolute rockstar.

At the end of the presentation, I entertained a brief question and answer period with Daryl Vaillancourt and the Ontario SPCA's communications guru, Emily Cook. When Daryl got to the microphone, he asked Kathy to come up to the stage with Kal, as well. Oh shit! Kathy asked me not to point her out, as she is very shy, and generally wanted to just blend in. During my presentation, I talk a lot about my family and especially Kathy, so her blending in was not happening. Kathy and Kal came on the stage and they presented Kal with a doggy bed, gave me a very nice gift and Kathy a bouquet of flowers. Kathy was on the stage beside me, the crowd was clapping; I was so proud of her.

After my presentation there was a refreshment break before the conference continued. Kathy and I walked down the stairs of the stage and there was a line up of people who wanted to thank me and some wanted to talk to me. The really cool thing was that while I had a line up of people who wanted to talk to me, so did Kathy. She was hugging people and answering questions about how she was doing, and how she was able to handle her husband struggling with PTSD and addiction. Her line was just as long as mine, and she stepped-up and spoke to all of them. This quiet little lady was thrust into a situation that was not expected, but she did a great job. Over the next two days of the conference, people continued to come up to both Kathy and me to talk or to thank us. We were both blown away by the affect my presentation had, and just how close Kathy and I were throughout this ordeal. After lunch, Kathy and I went to our room for some down time. I fell asleep, and Kathy read her book. Little did we know that this day was about to get even more special at the Celebration Dinner to come that evening.

As we settled into the formal Celebration Dinner in the grand hall, there was such a buzz in the room. Kathy and I were still being blessed by people coming up to talk to us to just chat. The compliments given to me for my candid presentation was an inspiration in my soul. As they say in the Grinch, "My heart grew". We sat at a table with Daryl Vaillancourt and other delegates of the conference; the hall was so beautiful, very impressive. The evening started with the usual dignitary words, little did I know it would turn into a moment in my life that I will never forget. I was becoming more confident and stronger before this event, but I felt so much stronger now, I was proud of myself for the first time in years.

Before the meal, my friend Mary Davis, joined by Board member Chris White, headed to the stage and grabbed the microphone. Their words were about to blow my mind, cause tears and create an even stronger Shawn. They went on to say that my presentation made an impact on everyone in the audience, so much so that the Ontario SPCA felt something needed to be done. On behalf of the Ontario SPCA, they wanted to sponsor the gift of a service dog. They wanted to help change the life of someone struggling with PTSD, just like I was. I mentioned during my talk that Kal came at a cost of approximately $20,000, a gift given to me by Nicole Simard and United by Trauma's fundraising. They then turned to the room and asked, "who wants to join in and sponsor a service dog for a first-responder or military member?" What happened next, I will probably never experience again. Immediately executive directors from SPCAs and Humane Societies from around Ontario, corporate partners, an Indigenous Community, and a few individual people, started putting up their hands, donating $500, $1000 and even $5000. In less than 5 minutes they raised $20,000 for another service dog. I was crying because I could not believe this was happening. As I am typing this story, I still get goose bumps. As Mary returned to her seat, I got up and gave her a huge hug, the crowd all clapped. It was such an emotional moment; a moment that would never have happened had I pulled the trigger in the change-room.

Afterwards, I was asked if I would head up this new endeavor, with Kal's trainer and United by Trauma for support, and connect someone with this unbelievable gift. I would work with my friend Daryl Vaillancourt at the Ontario SPCA and together we would help change the life of someone in need. I was honoured and touched beyond measure. United by Trauma, after providing support to many people in need through the gift of a service dog, were no longer active as a not-for-profit group. I still wanted to reach out to Nicole Simard, because without her and Kal, none of this would have been possible. She explained that she was in the process of training a black lab as a service dog and just could not take on any more projects at that time. She works full-time as an operating room nurse in the Greater Toronto Area, as well as many other selfless projects. She was supportive and as usual was the remarkable person I know her to be.

The next phone call I made was to Shai Perlmutter, the amazing dog trainer who trained Kal. I knew at this point that if I was to get involved with this project, Shai had to be my dog trainer. I am thankful he agreed to take on the project. My only stipulation was that I wanted no part in the formal contracts of money between Shai and the Ontario SPCA, and I did not want to be paid a cent. I wanted to volunteer my time and pay it forward to someone else. I owe a great deal of gratitude to the Ontario SPCA, especially Kate MacDonald, Daryl Vaillancourt and Mary Davis. This journey that began this night is still going on today. I have met so many wonderful people at the Ontario SPCA, and have had the opportunity to talk to other first responders and military members as a result. This project is of a personal nature to the recipients and to me as well, so I will not explain the project in too much detail. I will however tell you that the Ontario SPCA has all of the dogs and their handlers, recovering from PTSD, highlighted on their website in a series of blogs, videos and interviews. Please go check them out. To date, the Ontario SPCA has raised and donated $60,000 towards the purchase, training and delivery of 3 service dogs to people in need. I continue to be the volunteer lead, working with the Ontario SPCA and Shai Perlmutter, owner and head trainer of Evolution K9. Evolution K9 has a dynamic website as well, with stories of success in testimonials and videos.

My Daily Commitment to Recovery and Living Life

I still have bad days. Kal is a great help, but he is a part of my recovery plan. My full plan involves not only Kal, but also my support people. I have found that by living each day, choosing life, and trusting at least one person when in crisis, I have the keys to my success while in recovery. I have had multiple relapses, but I own them; with each one I set a new start day and get up and keep moving forward. I do not allow these brief lapses in judgement to dictate my future. I have learned that moments of crisis and moments of mental health instability are brief moments in time that can pass when handled with a proper plan. Equally, if I screw up, I never say, "I might as well just give in." I tell myself that I screwed up, and commit to moving forward again. I do not beat myself up, nor do I sit in the mess for a long period of time.

I have a dynamic family that fully supports me. The hardest part is telling others what is happening. I held it in for so many years, and it almost killed me. Once I chose to ask for help and explain what is going on, the most important people were there to support me. Stigma and shame were a part of the problem and caused me so much pain. It kept me sicker and hurting longer. As soon as I could wrap my mind around the fact that I was injured just like anyone else suffering a painful injury, I was able to shatter the shame, and not give a shit about the uneducated thoughts of others; thus, destroying stigma.

I was really dedicated to my sobriety in the earlier times after coming out of Homewood. I obtained a sponsor, I attended meetings and I read the literature. What I noticed in those rooms was a community and a family. Alcoholism and addiction can put their claws into anyone, regardless of social stature, money, career or fame. It had gripped this police officer, and understanding true humility was the key. I have been fortunate as well because my uncle, James Fougère has gone through what I am experiencing. When I reached out to James, I was looking for information, so that when I walked out of the doors of a treatment centre, or attended an event with alcohol, or experienced great joy or sadness, I knew what to expect, and how that might feel being sober. James has been a great role model and mentor to me. His message to me has always been clear, blunt and informative. If I have fallen, he has never judged, he continued to provide support. When I speak of my recovery plan and support people, he is right at the top of that list. I feel comfortable to call him and cry, swear or host a pity party; even just listening to his experiences has given me strength and hope. I am so blessed to have him in my life, he is integral to my success, and my ability to continue through the highs and lows of recovery.

The hardest part of addiction, for me, is that it never goes away. It has been said that the addiction demon is just waiting around the corner, doing push-ups, waiting for you to take that first drink, puff or injection. Each time I stumble, fail to use my systems, and walk with the demon, the darkness settles in faster. I have been in the program for over seven years now, and sadly, I have watched that demon take the lives of people I have met or destroyed any progress someone was cultivating for themselves. Addiction is a disease, and my program, family and work are my medicine. When I chose not take my medicine, the sickness returns.

I have been told that the addict or the alcoholic must choose to help themselves, that they cannot be saved or forced into sobriety. That is very true, and very scary. My family and support group pray for me, and support me, but if I listen to the demonic thoughts of my past traumas, and experience the sadness, I can easily fall. The addict or alcoholic must want to help themselves because the disease is very powerful. When I was suffering, I did not allow that support in, and it nearly caused my demise. However, on that sad day in May 2013, when my .40 calibre pistol was in my hand, my vision of Kathy, and the leap of faith to tell one person I trusted (Dean Ward), my journey of recovery began. I chose life that day, and trusted one person; that is my mantra and the key to my success.

The beautiful part of recovery is watching others succeed, and paying it forward, much like James Fougère did for me. I have met and spoke with many addicts living on the street, their lives in absolute shambles. I have seen them celebrate one month, one year and two years of sobriety from alcohol and/or drugs. I have watched the mother who lost her children because of addiction, be reunited with them. I have seen others rebuild their lives, find employment, housing and be happy. I have seen a lot more happiness within the walls of those rooms than sadness; the demon can be beaten, so long as we take it one day at a time.

I have had two local sponsors and each one of them has become a backbone for my recovery. Their guidance and teachings of the program helped me navigate all of the challenges of starting in recovery. The rooms are actually a very friendly place and a happy place; I shit you not. I see and hear more laughing and fellowship in those rooms than in most other public places. They are not scary; but what I needed was that guide, a sponsor. For people who do not know who to trust or who to talk to, I have watched countless newcomers pick up the phone and call the phone number for alcoholism or addiction. I know the people who answer those phones in North Bay, and they are caring, knowledgeable people who really care about the people calling. They will help you find meetings, and if needed, even provide you with a ride to a meeting, or a coffee to chat. The cool part is, it really is anonymous. Alcoholism and mental health injuries can be very hard to recover from, but I am telling you from the bottom of my heart, that you can become happy again. I have now turned 50 years old. I still have my family and have reached a level of happiness and gratitude I never thought possible. I did this by practicing humility, honesty, communication and a commitment to live life one day at a time. I am a success story, and I see countless stories of success everyday. I'll say it again, choose life and trust one person.

As I have mentioned before, I have seen many doctors with respect to my post traumatic stress disorder, both forced by the misguided system, and others while an inpatient. Together with my hard work, commitment and their expertise, I have grown, and established strategies to live one day at a time while suffering from mental health. Honesty in treatment and a willingness to believe in the process, in their guidance, and let go of the fear, have been the keys to success for me. Even with all the experts I have seen, I found myself stuck at a certain place. I needed a final nudge; I needed a different perspective and a different voice. During the summer of 2020, while at our camp in McKellar, Ontario, I began to research strategies online. I had heard of a process of treatment called EDMR (Eye Movement Desensitization and Reprocessing.) I have heard and read literature that this non-traditional type of psychotherapy has seen success for treating PTSD. As I researched the treatment, I began to read up on the providers in my area that offer this service. I read countless therapist summaries, trying to see if I could relate to any of them. I came across Centered Fire Counselling and Consulting – Brenda Quenneville, MSW, RSW. As I read her summary of services, she spoke of EDMR, but more importantly, as I read her synopsis, something inside of me clicked, and I knew I had to reach out to her. She provided the final nudge, and now I have reached a whole new level of peace and acceptance.

Brenda Quenneville responded to an email inquiry and agreed to meet with me. As we were in the middle of the COVID-19 pandemic, we met virtually via Zoom. Our first session was intense, in such a positive way. I immediately bonded with her, and felt a level of trust that was incredible. From August 2020, through to March 2021, we met virtually, weekly. Her process of EDMR strategies, lessons and her knowledge of how the brain responds was shared in a way that I was able to process. While I am not going to go over everything, just know she became my third-base coach. The baseball analogy of the third-base coach came from Brenda. When I was thanking her for how well I was feeling, she explained my recovery process like this: she explained that I had worked very hard not only with her, but with all of my previous treatment providers, and so far, I have been able to reach third-base. The issue was that I was stuck on third base and needed some direction to home plate. She was that third-base coach and gave me the final guidance I needed to touch home plate. She was so right. I have worked hard, and I have received some dynamic treatments over the years; her new approached moved me forward in my recovery journey.

Along with the hard work of EDMR therapy, her monologues to my inquiries were critical in my understanding of my roadblock with respect to full understanding of my PTSD. Some of the messages I received and resonated with were the keys to touching home plate. Brenda was able to explain that I was participating in "internal oppression". What this meant was that when I explained how I felt shame for not being at work, or needing a service dog, I was actually my own oppressor. During this discussion I realized that while I shattered shame to some degree, I held onto it as it related to my opinion about myself. When I looked in the mirror, I saw a broken and weak man. While others understood and were moving on, I subconsciously was not. Now I have been able to stop the self-shaming and work on my PTSD on a more personal level.

She explained that with PTSD, the way the brain is processing information, is "not a shameful pathology" of who I am, but the "natural way for the brain to work". Along with that bombshell, Brenda renamed the acronym of PTSD for me, and instant clarity after months of hard work with her occurred. She advised that the letter D, currently stood for Disorder. This word indicates a negative result of my injury, which in my case was assisting with my internal oppression. Brenda stressed that I change the D to R to stand for Post Traumatic Stress Response (PTSR). Simply put, my injury, as a result of past traumas my brain has endured, has produced a response that I need to understand and receive treatment for. That simple word change for me totally redirected how I felt about myself, and how I understood my triggers and symptoms of my past traumas. My mind was blown. The bottom line here is that I never gave up on myself, or stopped receiving treatments. Even though I was receiving great care from a great psychologist and psychiatrist, I felt something was missing something, and I needed to listened to myself. This drive to understand and recover to a new level, led me to Brenda. I owe a great deal to her talents, her knowledge and her training in helping me take this new step in my recovery.

CROSSROADS –
THE CHOICE IS YOURS

When I think about crossroads, I envision a cross-type roadway with a four-way stop. When I arrive at the crossroads, I have four choices, and every decision I make daily relies on my reflection of what each roadway means. To me, the roads are the paths I choose to follow. If I choose to turn around at the stop sign and retrace my steps, that is when I continue to sit in the mess of my past. This option leads me, generally, to follow past mistakes, and continue to make the same choices I always have. This familiar choice, while it may be perceived as easy, is the very past that has landed me at the crossroads in the first place. If I choose to go straight, this road leads me to my status quo, which has been a repetitive pattern of triggers, sobriety, relapses, apologetic professions and willingness myself to change my habits. Going straight has small periods of sanity, yet the cycle of mental health and addiction situations will more than likely cause an earlier death than I would like. If I turn left, I have given up entirely. A left turn means I no longer wish to try. I no longer have the ability to continue the fight and simply give in to my alcoholism, to numb the mental health injury and fog my mind from reality. This road will undoubtedly lead to my death, and more than likely at my own hands. Turning right, is the hardest road to take initially, but has the best possible long-term outcome.

Turning right is where I want to turn. This turn requires the use of the H-word, guidance, patience, and a commitment to recovery. I have turned right, but not without pain, conflict and at times, self-anger. Turning right is recovery; recovery is possible, beautiful and full of a life free of addiction. Right, now, is a cumulation of the past, mixed with the present; a present that, as the word itself can mean, is full of gifts. The future has yet to arrive, so I pay it no direct regard, because if I choose to live my life in the present, one day at a time, my future will be bright. A mouthful I hope you can understand. Living one day at a time, eventually amounts to many days, weeks, months, and years. Such a vision to this future can become overwhelming, but is most certainly attainable, living one day at a time.

While my career as a police officer can be viewed as the cause for my current state, it is a career that I am very proud of accomplishing. I have had so many positive moments as a police officer. Those positive moments are what I hold in my heart today. The repetitive traumas will always be in the past, but after working through them in treatment, I can now at least leave them there, and focus on my life now. That is what asking for help can do. I held onto to my shit for far too long, and if I had the benefit of hindsight, I would have asked for help a lot sooner. My dream for anyone, including first-responders, military and anyone else suffering a traumatic event, is that asking for help can be as normal as asking for help for a sore ankle, an infection or a life-threatening physical ailment. Imagine a life where employers, friends, families and the social media pundits of the world, accept a few days off to rest, reflect and seek treatment for a mental ailment. To me, it is a no-brainer; if we can accept an illness or injury as anything that affects the body or mind, and be given the treatment and acceptance of recovery, we will all be the better for it.

I want to touch on two life changing events I have experienced in a positive way as a police officer, so I can end this narrative on a positive note. Like I mentioned, I am proud of the work I have done as a police officer with the OPP. I have many instances where I have been proud of my work, but I will focus on two.

On February 15th, 2008, while I was on patrol, I came to the intersection of Highway #17 and Gormanville Road in North Bay, where I observed vehicles stopped and parked all over the highway. I turned on my emergency lights and exited my vehicle where I was approached by a male who said he just hit a pedestrian and she was laying on the highway not moving. I ran to where this young woman was lying, she was unconscious, non-responsive, and even worse, not breathing. As I was assessing her, two other officers arrived on the scene. Working together, we carefully rolled her onto her back, I held her head and cervical spine to prevent further injuries while the other officers rolled her over with precision. Once she was on her back, the airway which was previously blocked, assumingly due to positional asphyxia, opened and she took a deep breath. Even though she was unconscious, her body began to react to pain, and she became agitated and was trying to move about. Our job now was to keep her still so she would not exacerbate any possible injuries. She was transported to the hospital by ambulance and later flown to a Toronto-area hospital. She was hospitalized for quite a time and would endure a painful recovery.

Since that day, this young woman, Emily Pearson, has kept in contact with me as a sign of her gratitude. The other officers and I involved in her care received a Life Saving Award at a ceremony in Cobalt, Ontario. Emily and her parents made the trip and she was a part of the presentation. Emily is the picture of bravery, strength and determination and I am very grateful for how things worked out that day. Emily has since graduated from teachers' college, married and given birth to two beautiful children. Every year on February 15th, we have a conversation by text, and it warms my heart. She does not live in the North Bay area, but whenever she is close by she calls me and we meet for a coffee or lunch with her awesome young family. This incident is the reason why I became a police officer; to help people. While I most certainly did not do it alone, being a part of a team dedicated to helping people, and on this day helping Emily, gives me a memory of satisfaction and pride of the uniform.

The second story I want to share involves a family member by marriage, who everyday shows the gratitude that most people have for first responders. Patrick Gaudreault, who is my wife's cousin, is an amazing young man. Patrick suffered through post-meningitis trauma when he was five-months old. His mom shared that the fluid around his brain had become infected as a result of the meningitis and had squeezed his brain leaving him what has been diagnosed as mentally delayed. Patrick operates at the level of a nine year old for some things, and his birthday age for others. Patrick is an awesome human, someone we should all strive to be like. He is funny, energetic, loves all around him, and he calls himself my back-up. Patrick loves the police, fire fighters, and ambulance attendants. He thinks the vehicles, emergency features of the vehicles, the uniforms, and the people who wear them, are great. If Patrick sees any one of those people, in or out of their vehicle, he wants to say, "Hi!" and will tell you how much he appreciates them.

When I first met Patrick, before I was married or a police officer, he was a young lad who possessed a love of life that was infectious to everyone around him. His parents, Kim and Hormidas Gaudreault, who also had a daughter at home, were remarkable, as well. As the years ticked by, and Patrick grew into an adult, he began to experience health issues that were very serious. He was hospitalized for months, and in some incidences he has had to travel to various hospitals across Ontario. Through it all, Patrick remained Patrick. Whenever I saw Patrick, he wanted to talk police-talk. He wanted me to know that people were speeding on his road and it was not safe. He would discuss scenarios that he could help me as my back-up. I absolutely love this young man. I have given him as much OPP paraphernalia as I could find, from hats, clothes and I even designed him his own wallet badge, with a badge number of 8330A. My badge number was 8330. I have taken him on ride-alongs in my police car, and thanks to our marine officer, had him out on our police boat as well. He loves the outdoors, and he lives in the country with family as his neighbours. His uncles and aunts have worked so hard to create kilometres of trails behind his house. He uses them all the time. He goes out with his dedicated family almost daily. I have brought my ATV to his house and went for rides, just him and I, and I even let him drive. I would sit on the back of the bike and Patrick would navigate the ATV amongst the trees, rocks and curves with precision and safety. He could teach a safety course. Patrick is the type of person everyone needs in their life.

A few years ago, during one of Patrick's lengthy hospital stays I received a call from his mom, Kim. She advised that he was not doing well and there was a possibility he could die. I went to go see him in the hospital. His body was failing him and the hospital staff were not able to help him. He was hooked up to hospital machines, he was weak and for the first time, I did not see Patrick smile. When I walked in, although happy to see me, I could tell he was in pain.

I came up with an idea. The one thing this young man loved more than anything was the police, and he would love to be a police officer. I went to pay a visit to our Chief Superintendent Scott Tod. Scott Tod, who has since retired from the OPP and is now the Chief of the North Bay Police Service, is an incredible man. He was an example of one of the great OPP leaders we had. The OPP dropped a peg in the executive ranks when he walked out the door. He led by example, had a great work ethic, a positive attitude, and he always looked after everyone under his command. He had the ability to lead this difficult field of service, while making people feel important and valued. He proved positive and supportive leadership was possible within the OPP. I asked the Chief if we could swear Patrick in as a Special Constable with the OPP. He not only agreed, but had an official looking document drawn up and wanted to be there to swear him in. We arranged a time, and I met him and his two superintendents in Patrick's room. Chief Tod read the document and Patrick was now a sworn Special Constable for that day. Then in an unexpected act of kindness, the Chief gave Patrick his Chief Superintendent Peak Police Cap. Patrick was beyond touched and proud. He wanted us to sign the inside of the hat for him; so along with the Chief and the two Superintendents, this Constable signed the hat as well.

Within a few days of his swearing in, the hospital tried a new drug to treat his health condition and it began to work. He was diagnosed with aggressive Crohn's Disease, resulting in many health-related conditions, including a colostomy bag called a stoma appliance. Fortunately, Patrick walked out of that hospital. The kid who loved life and loved everyone, walked out with his signature smile, thanking the hospital staff he left behind. He is amazing. Patrick still has to go in for medical procedures, and there are maintenance tasks that his mom has to help him with at home, but Patrick is now 32 years old, and back to his regular self. Patrick has been blessed in many ways, but to have the parents he has is probably his biggest gift. His mother in particular, is an absolute rockstar; she works, cares for her family and runs the household; the definition of a strong woman.

To battle through mental health ailments with addiction, or without, can seem like hiking Mt. Everest barefoot, but it can be managed. The biggest take away I wish for anyone who reads this book is to feel a sense of hope that in that moment of darkness, others will have the strength to choose life and trust one person. The road can be rough, as it is with many illnesses, injuries or diseases, but that road is never blocked completely. Turn right, talk to someone and believe in yourself; bet on your future.

Learning to love yourself is the biggest challenge when you are sitting alone in the dark. Look in the mirror, in daylight, and tell yourself you are worth life and a life in recovery. Do this everyday, even if you do not believe it at first; fake it until you make it!

Epilogue

The freedom I have discovered from writing this book has been as much of a surprise to me as it has been integral to a part of my recovery. I have learned so much and continued to grow over the last few years and I want to provide you all with a final snapshot of how I am, and how my recovery is going now, after having completed this book.

I never thought it would be possible but, I have peace today. When I reflect on the past and see the darkness, the pain and the embarrassment that I was feeling, I am astounded and overjoyed about the life I have today. I have a greater sense of peace and a quality of life that I am enjoying, but I do not think I will ever say that I am cured. I continue to participate in counselling, take medications, and I need to be aware of my triggers and events that require coping mechanisms, to get me through each day safely. PTSD is here to stay. This brain injury I accumulated over my career as a police officer is part of my life, but I can now say that I am in relative control of it, instead of it running my life.

It has been through my recovery process that I have begun to let go of the anger and resentment that has kept me sick for so much longer than it should have. I will never be able to forget the damage the OPP managers have caused to my well being, but I am now able to put it all behind me. I hope that those insensitive, archaic and pathetic people will one day be able to see what their ignorance has cost my family and me. I only wanted to be heard, to be appreciated and to be understood; sadly they all failed me. When I see them on the street, I will not wave or even acknowledge them, but know that because of the love of those around me, and the work that I have put in, I have made it through to the other side. I will never forget, nor will I forgive, but I am at a place to say that my past is behind me, and my future is full of love and hope.

I have learned so much about the human brain through counselling, experts, readings and practising recovery methods. I have learned that the brain, when injured and untreated, can kill. However, this same brain can heal itself just like any other part of the body that has been injured. It takes work, guidance, and a tenacious drive. When my world was dark, and my brain was on life support, I was gifted with a moment of clarity, a vision of my wife, that I did not ignore. It was the first time I told myself to choose life and trust one person. That is quite simply why I am alive today.

What I have learned, and my message to anyone, is to recognize your brain injury, or those moments of trauma, and deal with them head on and right away. Educate yourself on treatment and recovery processes with the experts in the field. Have strength of perseverance and do not feel shame, because there is never shame when you face issues of the brain with strength. My life was worth saving, and because I was able to survive that one moment in time, I am now enjoying more time, in peace. I have had many great friends and family members to surround myself with, once I allowed them in. I have a sponsor right now, Rick, who has lived, experienced and is willing to share his strength and hope with me, and quite frankly anyone who wants to chat. Not long ago, Rick explained the significance of a life to me this way. He said that a very wise man he loved and respected told him, while looking at a headstone in a graveyard, that the dash (-) between the date you were born and the date that you died was the most important marking on the granite. He explained that the beginning and the ending do not really matter, but what you did with the dash is what was really important. My dash is still in progress, and I now know that is where my legacy should be focused.

Alcoholism and addiction on their own are extremely difficult to recover from, that is why they are a disease. I have spoken about the good people who succumb to this disease. Once the disease grips you, and gets activated organically, chemically and physically within your body and soul, the fight for your life literally begins. I continue to fight this fight and I will for the rest of my life. The linkage between my PTSD and alcoholism is so intwined that they begin to feed each other, blurring the lines of which trigger or battle you are experiencing at a given time. When

I am under the influence of alcohol, I want all the alcohol I can get. Once I introduce this chemical into my body and mind, the madness ignites. The once gleeful feeling I had from a good drunk, is now replaced with a need to drink just to function or escape within myself. My mind and thought process while under the influence are downright dangerous. I am no more the funny drunk man; I have become my own worst enemy. These chemicals are a threat to my very life. They heighten mental health triggers and confuse my recovery plans and treatment strategies. It angers me, makes me resentful of all that has wronged me, and now literally has changed me. Drunk Shawn is a danger to everything I hold dear. He threatens my peace, he threatens my relationships, he threatens my actions and reactions, and he ultimately threatens my life. I know all of this and yet there are still times that I drink. Why? It is a disease; it is my go-to response when triggered. It activates my body, and especially my mind, so that it feels essential. I can have a bottle of vodka or a beer in my hand before I have even thought of the purchase. I have also yelled at myself all the way to the liquor store to stop, only to walk in, and buy what I feel is the serum for my soul. I repeat all of what the alcohol threatens that I mentioned above, only to chug the vodka like a quenching sports drink. Am I weak, or stupid, or asking for it? No, I am not, and neither is anyone addicted to alcohol or drugs. We are sick, and often really want to stop, especially when a point is reached where our physical body is about to tap out.

The addiction is just as dangerous as my mental health injury. These two fatalistic diseases and injuries run amok inside my brain everyday trying to see who will break me first, or at least that is how bad it used to be. I would love to tell you that since I left the Homewood Treatment Centre in July of 2013, I have been sober. Sadly, I cannot. What I can tell you is that to this day, I do not want to drink and I want to live in peace; a peace that quiets my PTSD. It is this attitude that makes me a success. What I need to remember, and most importantly process everyday, is that alcohol consumption makes things worse and is not a happy, comforting place to be. I have enough negative situations and experiences with alcohol now to write a book about that. I need to work, think and use my sobriety program everyday, along with talking to Rick everyday. The COVID-19 pandemic has been very hard on everyone. The pandemic has impacted my treatment regiment by closing the rooms of recovery, and cutting-off social contact with the very people I need. These beautiful people, who know exactly how I feel, how I think and what I need, are no longer there the way they used to be. I hate the phone, I always have. I think Zoom is a great platform for some events, but I cannot use Zoom for sobriety meetings. I feel like I am on a goofy set-up of the Hollywood Squares. If I am not comfortable, then I do not share or listen and I shut down.

Hurdles, there will always be hurdles. It is the mindset, the program, the fellowship and the contact of like minds that I need. When I first admitted I was an alcoholic and I reached out for help, I was beyond depressed. I was so down that instead of looking at my alcoholism as a life-threatening disease, I threw a pity party. I imagined not being able to ever drink again, at weddings, funerals, graduations, birthdays, sports, family gatherings, camping, fishing, birth of a child, promotion, moving, and so on. Can you imagine what that feels like? Think about this right now. I just told you, you can never drink alcohol again, not because you do not want to drink, but because you just can't, because you are not like normal people with alcohol. When you look at sobriety like this, it is no surprise the failure rate can be relatively high. When battling PTSD and using alcohol as a cure serum, the weight becomes even more unbearable.

From about Christmas 2020 to July 2021, I began to drink again. I forgot everything I knew and fell into the grasp of addiction again. Everything was piling up, and I made a mistake; a mistake I do not even remember making. For about four and a half months, I was drinking again. I picked up right where I left off, and this time, I wanted more. I so wanted to have the fairy tale story of good guy makes it, so it fueled the pity party a little while longer. The difference though was that I was informed and experienced, and now do want to live a peaceful and sober life. I had a taste of it, and I loved it. I involved my family, as well as Rick, and met this regression head on. Coincidentally, I had a doctor's appointment within a couple days of my declaration, and of course my doctor asked how my sobriety was going. I was honest with her. She is a very professional and no-nonsense doctor. She cares for people; my family and I are very fortunate to have her. We have developed a follow up plan which enabled me to be accountable to her, and she offered me the resources and support I needed. Honesty is another H-word that helps.

This last sort of summary was a final opportunity I wanted to take to share all of my story. Mental health issues are real, and addiction is dangerous. I am not ashamed of either one. My family walks beside me, because they see how hard I try and work to be the best Shawn I can be everyday. I can do this by being honest, and committing daily to my recovery plans. These will always include choosing life and trusting one person.

Made in the USA
Las Vegas, NV
19 August 2022